Where's the Designer?

Peter Seddon

BBC Television Training

First published in 1993 by
BBC Television Training
BBC Elstree Centre
Borehamwood
Hertfordshire

© 1993 BBC Television Training
All rights reserved
ISBN 0 948694 01 7

A CIP catalogue record for
this book is available from
the British Library

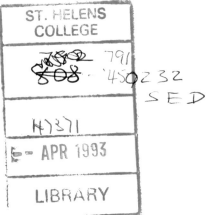
General Editor:
Gordon Croton

Design and production:
Shirley Greenfield

Photographs:
John Barrett p.139

Drawings & plans for *The Secret Agent*:
Michael Trevor

Shot size diagrams and 'Expanding Horizons':
Nick Skelton p.44 and 149

Printed by
Able Printing Ltd
Paddock Wood
Kent
England

Contents

4

6

Acknowledgements

The experience I have gained over a long period in television design is the result of working with many different producers, directors and production teams on a wide variety of programmes and later as Head of Television Design watching other designers at work and learning from them, as well as meeting colleagues from other companies and countries to compare notes.

This extended process makes the task of mentioning individual names a virtual impossibility; however, I should like to pay special tribute to all the television designers I met during my time at the BBC who were united in striving for the best possible results whatever the challenge and wherever they were.

I should like to thank Gordon Croton and Shirley Greenfield at BBC Television Training for the invitation to write this book and for their help and support in its preparation.

INTRODUCTION

A Question of Design

It is a curious contradiction that designers' offices, (ranging in appearance from clinic-like complexes with the latest computer to the plain untidy) do, for a large part of the time, also turn out to be empty. Over the years this phenomenon has been observed by production teams, and indeed designers themselves, as being the one constant and unchanging factor that serves to distinguish the many design departments and individual design offices around the world.

"Where's the designer?" is a question frequently heard within the production team, specially during the busy build-up to a studio recording or location shoot. There is a clear inference that once the designer has been found, there will be a lot more questions to be posed and answered. For this reason it provides a good title, a starting point and a framework through which to explore the world of television design and the television production designer. It is hoped that a clearer image will emerge of the potential benefits to producers and directors of having a good designer working on their programmes and by extension a better informed notion of where to start looking the next time the cry goes up in the production office "where's the designer?"

This book is intended to explain the process of television production design to three main groups of readers:

To potential television designers and design students by looking briefly at:

- The development of television design and some of the influential factors that have changed its direction over the past 25 years.
- Various types of production on which the designer works with examination of how individual programmes call for similar yet distinct design responses.
- The design process.

- Training for television designers today. The evolving National Vocational Qualifications, and specifically the Skillset lead body for film, broadcast and video, provide an important pointer for the future of the industry by setting up the infrastructure necessary to implement the television industry's new standards and required criteria. NVQs analyse the key functions of the role of a television production designer, as well as indicating the direction and emphasis required from designers of tomorrow.

To production teams:

- By giving an idea of the potential scope and involvement of production design.
- By indicating the nature of the design advice that can be available to programme makers during the creative process of planning and realisation of their programmes.

To students of the media
and any readers who are interested in the process of design realisation as an integral part of the process of television production.

Chapter 1

Background:
The Development of Television Design

When the BBC launched the first regular public service television service in 1936, its first priority was to establish a firm technical foundation, built by its engineering expertise, in order to ensure that the new system was reliable. Nevertheless, in a very short time it was also looking for design help to give television its own particular visual identity as distinct from theatre or film. Initially in the BBC there were two designers, whose previous experience had been in film and theatre respectively; when television resumed after the war, it was from these same design backgrounds that the early television designers were recruited.

From the early 1950s onwards, television began to develop its own designers, as it was obvious that neither film nor theatre techniques were, for different reasons, appropriate for the new medium. In theatre scenery, the quality of detail and painting was devised to be viewed by the human eye from a reasonable distance and in a controlled and subdued lighting condition, whereas the (relatively) harsh, bright light required for the all-seeing television camera would have rendered such an effect completely inappropriate and even tawdry. In film scenery, the composite yet fragmented sets, usually built *in situ* with magnificent and heavy detail, lit for and shot by a single camera in a much slower timescale, were not the right answer for the fast-changing multi-camera output of television. Television was encouraged to develop its own specialised designers by an increasing audience coupled with fast improving equipment and facilities.

Designers' backgrounds and training

Over the years of its relatively brief history, design backgrounds and experience within television design have changed extensively from the early '50s. Then, designs were undertaken by people recruited solely from the worlds of theatre and film and as the demand for a clearer visual image of the television output grew, through its development period in the '50s and early '60s, Richard Levin as Head of Design at the BBC, for the first time specifically invited into television designers from architecture, interior design and exhibition design for the very purpose of bringing their influences to bear on the screen image. As a result, the number and variety of designers gradually grew to include nearly all the art and design disciplines that could be found on offer in an art college, polytechnic or university. Not only did the academic backgrounds change and expand, but so did the nature of the work. The design opportunities that were offered with the arrival in 1964 of BBC2 meant improved picture quality of 625 lines. The introduction in 1967 of colour, and then the gradual filtering in of computers and digital video effects all allowed the designer to work on a much broader canvas and at a higher level of definition and sophistication than had ever been possible before.

The advent of ITV
With the creation of Independent Television or Commercial Television in 1955, there was a sudden movement of staff from the BBC as a number of new ITV companies set up their own design departments and, in the process, drew on experienced BBC designers to help staff their new organisations. Battle lines were drawn between public service broadcasters on the one hand and the commercial companies on the other; at the time this divide was real, and it is only in retrospect that the overall combined output of BBC and ITV is considered, without much argument, as being public service television despite the commercial nature of the ITV companies themselves.

Design standards
In the early 60s, the threat of commercialisation and the need for greater audiences was seen by many as counter to the maintenance of creative standards in programme making. At the time it was considered by BBC designers to be a real threat to the continuation of aesthetic standards and was a factor that directly influenced designers entering the world of television when they decided whether to work in the public or commercial sector.

It is interesting to draw a comparison between the unquestioned and almost instinctive concern for professional and aesthetic standards in the '60s and '70s with the recent debate brought about by the 1990 Broadcasting Act concerning the 'quality' of television programmes. Politicians, bureaucrats and programme makers alike now appear to find it difficult to define what precisely *does* constitute quality in a legislative context.

Through the late '50s, right into the '70s, in the BBC and ITV (and also in many organisations around the world who chose to model their systems to a greater or lesser extent on what they saw in Britain) design departments were developed and maintained on an implicit belief in realising the highest possible visual standards on the screen whilst working within the given budgetary limits. This concern grew in an atmosphere that demanded, and was conducive to, new and exciting ideas. More important still, all this creative activity took place at a time when the financial demands generated by these ideas could still be met out of existing income, without too much trouble. The custodians of visual standards in television were *de facto* the design departments and their designers rather than the producers and directors. It was their professional advice and experience that determined to a large extent the size of pro-ducers' cash budgets and the amount of resources that were allocated by the programme planners.

The introduction of colour
The introduction of colour in 1967 brought with it a sudden shift of emphasis in the television design world, as costumes imme-diately assumed far greater importance than had been the case in the past. This was due to the fact that there was the new phenomenon of a naturalistic looking (rather than black and white) face to look at and because the costumes occupied a very significant part of the screen area immediately surround-ing the face of the actor or presenter. Consequently, costumes occupied the screen and the viewers' attention for a far greater proportion of the time than had been the case hitherto, when the grammar of television direction had imposed vista-style long shots in which costumes made less of a direct impact.

With the advent of colour television, it was essential that the design, colour and texture of the costumes were 'right', as they suddenly attracted a great deal of attention on the television screen, much to the delight of the costume designers who welcomed the opportunity with open arms. The addition of colour to the recently improved definition of the 625-line black and white picture had a momentous and almost mesmerising effect on viewers and programme makers alike. Many so-called costume dramas were made in the rush to exploit to the full this new-found spectacle; now it was possible to see the human face in more or less natural tones, and the closest surroundings to the human face were the costumes; they suddenly had to be made to specific designs manufactured to a new and much higher quality in order to stand up to the closer scrutiny and their immediate comparison with the human face. Costume designers grew in confidence, number, status and importance — not least due to the increased costs of specially making or hiring the costumes — and the television production designer had for the first time to design the sets in a manner that was carefully related to the colour and style of the costumes than had ever been necessary in the monochrome past.

Computers and digital video effects

The gradual introduction of computers and digital video effects into television technology also had a very significant effect on television production design by enabling the use of composite images through inlay and overlay techniques which were used in a far more complex manner than had been possible earlier. The use of chromakey (or CSO in the BBC) enabled the use of inlay in conjunction with glass, matte and model shots to achieve early design effects.

Since the mid-80s, the use of CAD (computer aided design) in production design has been developed gradually in the BBC, first at Pebble Mill, where John Plush, a member of the design staff wrote a custom built software programme for designers; then later by a team at Television Centre, employing the use of both 2D surface modeller and 3D solid modeller computer packages to create models and plans and then to predict camera shots by the use of accurate storyboards. Suddenly it became possible to predict with great accuracy what would be seen through a given camera lens from a specified camera position within a particular aspect ratio. This facility had the added benefit of being able to produce accurate matte lines that were completely reliable when designing composite images on the television screen which had, of necessity, to be shot in different locations, (often at different times) and some time later be edited together with studio sequences.

A digital paint system was also linked to the CAD facility at Television Centre, enabling complex matte shots to be achieved by design staff in a variety of circumstances. It was used in conjunction with the CAD facility and operated by a small group of dedicated staff. In the ITV companies there were two CAD systems in use for a similar period of time, but they did not become established to the same extent.

Elsewhere in the world, for example at NHK in Tokyo, CAD systems are linked with digital paint systems and also with 3D computer graphics systems, while in Canada and Finland electronic scenery is already in use. In Ireland, Italy, Sweden and Denmark, as well as the USA, there are variations of CAD systems being established and used in a variety of ways.

Although these techniques are not easy to use at first hand, and often need expert operators in order to obtain the best results within given time limits, the visual possibilities provided have nevertheless developed steadily and in parallel with the further reaching changes and faster developing facilities of the computer graphics world.

Computer graphics
Computer graphics is a term which covers several different component parts of the graphic designer's work, e.g. film animation, video rostrum systems, digital paint and modelling systems, stills stores, digital effects and character generators; it can also be used as a generic term to cover all or any of them. Either way, computer graphics has provided both a larger palette as well as a more receptive canvas for the graphic designer to work on, and has increased the visual possibilities

available to programmes not only in far more complex title sequences than was possible in the past, but particularly in the area of programme content.

Another very important factor to have emerged is that the cost of these facilities has meant that graphic designers have assumed a position of greater artistic and financial significance in both corporate and programme terms. Rather than being asked, as was often the case, to design a title sequence *after* the sets and costumes had been commissioned and paid for, the availability of these new facilities and the possibilities they opened up meant that graphic designers began to be consulted by producers and directors at a far earlier stage in the programme-making process.

Similarly, in capital investment terms, corporations and companies began to include sums of money for the development of various aspects of computer graphic equipment. Another source of funding for computer graphics came from the general election programme budgets, as BBC and ITV competed strongly for viewers during the one-night stand of election coverage.

The effect of this major development in computer graphics on the production designer in television was similar to that experienced when colour ushered in a new role and era for the costume designer. Although it has to be said that in the case of costume designers this development was relatively short-lived (there are far fewer costume designers working in television today than in the '60s and '70s because of the demise of period drama), the role and scope of the graphic designer is likely to go on developing even further, especially in the use of electronically generated environments. In many current affairs and documentary programmes, for example, computer graphics title sequences can successfully suggest strong images and impressions of the programme content, so that at the end of the title sequence, it is appropriate for the studio environment to relate directly to the already established graphic design of the programme.This has been another new situation for the production designer who until this development had been used to providing the initial design input expressed through the design of the studio, rather than following the style set by a colleague. The new possibilities offered by computer graphic developments call for a greater spread of responsibility and closer teamwork in order to achieve a co-ordinated and integrated design for the production.

The demise of studio drama

Another significant factor of change to affect the working of the production designer occurred in 1984 when the BBC decided that the major proportion of its drama output would be made on film. This decision signalled the virtual end of electronic studio drama production as it had been developed from the '50s and nowadays it is difficult to find one major drama being shot in an electronic studio despite the many advances in cameras and their mountings, digital video effects and recording techniques.

A major part of the base on which so much of the design work from the 50s to the 70s was founded, namely a large number of studio-based drama productions — a whole host of plays series and serials — that called for the accumulated experience skills and traditions built up by a complex team of studio technicians, suddenly began to disappear as the main demand for their skills had ceased. The scale of the move from studio to location meant a big reduction in the opportunity to practise studio drama skills which until then had represented a high point of expression, not only for the designer but also for most of the other technicians.

The growth of location drama

This move away from studio recording presented a greater opportunity for designers to work on location — which in itself was not new as many productions in the past had used filmed or videotaped inserts to be played into studio recordings. To many designers this was a preferred course of action, as there was always a far better team spirit and working relationship on location than it was ever possible to generate in the electronic studios. However, it brought the need to develop essentially different design and servicing responses and techniques which were required when working on location where unforeseen delays and time loss could be horrendously expensive.

Although in the electronic studio and on film the essence of programme making is pre-planning, it is nevertheless true that once on location the designers and production teams have to rely far more on their own individual initiatives, usually without the extensive support of a large organisation or company to solve their production problems for them, as would tend to be the case with an in-house studio production. Production teams and designers have to respond to many unforeseen problems that occur in spite of the most meticulous pre-planning imaginable. The essence of the job on location is to be able to respond positively and creatively to ever-changing demands made under the increasing pressures of time and money.

Film, television and video

Today, as the distinction between designing for film, network television and video is becoming less and less clear; the same designers can be found working at different times on location or in a studio, on video or film, for a network company, a corporate video company or indeed an independent film. Films are being made for television, but with planned theatric release; sometimes large-scale television projects can have budgets that come close in scale to those of some films. Corporate video calls for a different scale of operation with tighter costs and production demands that are correspondingly more pragmatic. TV commercials, on the other hand, can cost considerably more to produce than the programme that precedes or follows them. Despite this wide-ranging scale of activities, values and costs, the underlying design skills required are fundamentally the same, and gradually the difference between what were three distinct fields of media design (i.e. film, video and network television) is diminishing due to the changing circumstances in the television and video world.

Unlike some other countries, such as Finland, Denmark, Sweden, Norway, Japan, Korea, Holland and Poland, where designers are expected to operate across the boundaries of the different media, there is in the UK relatively little interchange between designers for the theatre and those in film and television. A few designers do work in all three areas but they are small in number and when they do it is usually the result of having worked successfully with a director or producer in one of the other fields.

The production designer in television today

More than ever before designers in television, film or video have to be ready to respond to a variety of challenges that could come from any one of a number of different directions. The situation facing them now is vastly different from that of old — it is changing much more quickly and moving in a radical direction. In order to reduce overheads and improve on corporate efficiency, design and other servicing departments in the BBC and ITV are being steadily reduced in size as their work load diminishes and changes as more independent productions are made. This trend is likely to continue in the future. In the BBC, the introduction of Producer Choice and the direct competition it brings between staff and freelance designers, will add to the pressure that is building up against the survival of craft departments.

In the mid '70s, designers worked within the patronage and confines of established television institutions, safe in the knowledge that network television could continue to fill their time with predominantly home produced programmes of an interesting and demanding mix viewed from a design perspective. The story today is very different. Unremitting financial forces are causing radical changes to be implemented throughout television. A fundamental shift of responsibility is taking place and decision-making is being devolved from corporate management to the individual producer, who now has greater choice on the question of which technicians and resources to use. The consequence of this will be a reduction in support services that previously existed for the help and support of all programmes rather than just the short term needs of a single producer's programme under current realisation.

A key question that remains to be answered is whether these reduced levels will be able to generate a breakeven in the support services when in competition with freelances. Unrealistically high overheads (attributable to earlier eras) mean that financial viability is unlikely to be achieved; if so, and further reductions take place, the various craft skills will be in danger of further fragmentation and dilution.

During the '60s and '70s, design departments (managers and designers) had influenced the overall design costs of a production to a greater degree than producers; programme budgets were assembled by the planning department of an organisation dispensing resources across the whole programme plan, rather than a production accountant working in the interests of an individual producer. The effect of inherited corporate budgets on producers (and indirectly on other members of the team including designers), was to develop a questioning attitude towards budgetary responsibility as being something that could be accepted if it seemed reasonable, or if it did not, as sometimes happened, collectively evaded.

Leaving aside the effects of financial and political changes for a moment, a further effect of the present changes is the possibility of greater specialisation. Whereas in the past designers in the design departments of television companies were encouraged to work in several different areas of programme making, in order to become all-rounders and therefore more easily allocated by design managers to a wider range of programmes, the introduction of more independent productions and freedom of choice by producers means that it is likely to be far more difficult for a designer or design manager to plan very much direction into a career, be it staff or freelance. Until an invitation comes there is little decision to be made and, when it does, if there is no other work available there is no alternative but to accept. Consequently designers are likely to become experts in what they have been asked to design.

The other main point of difference being experienced by designers and programme makers alike is the transfer of responsibility that is gradually taking place from corporate level — responsibility for all the programmes being made — to individual producers and their programmes. While this transition is taking place there will be grey areas of shared responsibility between the organisation and the individual programme that make clear cut responsibility for finance and resources as difficult to achieve as it is desirable.

Where does design work take place?

Not only is the nature of work changing but designers are now expected to work in a greater variety of venues than previously. In the '60s, television designers worked almost entirely in electronic studios, usually an all-purpose studio (that could be used with equal facility by drama, light entertainment, music, talks and current affairs) of average size — approximately 8000 square feet — equipped with as many of the latest technological facilities as capital development programmes would allow. Acoustically treated, with extensive scenic, electrical and mechanical facilities, scene crew, props and construction standby rooms (to say nothing of the facilities required for all the other design and technical areas such as costume, make-up, visual effects and so on, they represented the state of the art work-place for designers and programme makers. Only occasionally was film used as an insert to programmes and then on a small scale, because there were considerable visual problems of matching film to tape and film to studio conditions.

Today the term 'studio' can cover any number of different combinations and levels of facilities that can be hired by the day according to the needs of a particular production — 'Wet or Dry Hire' involves the hire of technical facilities with or without operational personnel. Independent studios have existed for many years servicing independent productions, such as films, commercials, educational and corporate videos but until recently have not been extensively used by designers in the BBC and ITV companies. This situation is changing now, partly due to the increase of independent productions and the realisation that it is possible to make programmes in smaller studios that may not have all the built-in facilities of the BBC and ITV, but are nevertheless suitable for the progammes being made in them. The increased number of independent productions has meant that gradually BBC and ITV designers are being drawn into the world of rented facilities and different work practices, with the result that their experience is broadened and they have the opportunity to look at their own internal facilities and practices in a new light.

Where are the sources of design work?
The main sources of work for production designers in the UK are still the BBC and ITV companies. However, an increasing amount of freelance effort is being used and both organisations are actively engaged in reducing their staffing levels.

Video is being used increasingly in the leisure industry, in museums, theme parks and arts centres, at point of sale displays in the retail sector, as well as for public relations events, rock and pop concerts and for corporate communication. This wide ranging list contains within it a tremendous variety of demand for the designer, with a differing scale of operation (design requirement, budget and time) as well as the need for different approaches and practices from the production team.

Where is television made?
Television productions and videos are made today in a wide variety of places and circumstances and it might be useful to examine some of these in order to illustrate the range of facilities that a designer is likely to encounter.

STUDIOS
Under the term 'studios' is included the purpose built 'in-house television studios' designed with the intention of providing the best possible all-round facilities at the time they were planned. These differ from most studios that are available for hire in that they attempt to cater for as many different eventualities as possible — full-scale drama, entertainment, music, without the need to hire supplementary equipment on the day.

Independent studios, on the other hand, aim to hire out their facilities to individual production companies who have neither the wish nor the need to possess their own studios. Their aim is to provide basic, but flexible facilities, based on a rate card, that will offer an attractive proposition from both organisational and financial standpoints. It is often far more efficient to book a studio for a shoot rather than to have a unit trying to film on location, battling against the vagaries of the weather, parking, catering and travelling.

Such studios can be found with many different levels of facility and electronic recording and editing equipment. Some simply have a bare working space (which may or may not be sound-proofed) for drive-in use and equipment can be hired with or without operators according to the requirements of the individual productions renting them. There are also film stages, such as those at Pinewood, Elstree, Shepperton, Bray and Twicken-ham, each with their surrounding but largely independent support services.

OUTSIDE LOTS

Outside lots are sometimes used by television companies and are no more than suitably-sized outdoor spaces, on which permanent sets can be built to stand for considerable lengths of time. Examples of these can be seen at BBC Elstree where the *Eastenders* and *Grange Hill* programmes both use exterior lot facilities, and at Granada, the home of *Coronation Street,* and a lot which includes the Baker Street of Sherlock Holmes or the specially built *Brookside* of Redmond Productions for Channel 4.

The advantages of a permanent lot are obviously in the readily available facilities at an existing base, but it is equally possible to establish a permanent set away from company premises but with its own self-sufficient facilities. Either way the benefits lie in the reduced travelling time and better organisation of the schedule. From a design point of view the main point of concern is the provision of real time continuity — props and sets generally do not have to be struck and re-set and far greater attention can be paid to details of visual continuity which are so important in good quality soap operas.

The photographs on pages 33-38 illustrate well the setting up and shooting on a lot, and were taken during the making of the BBC's *The Secret Agent*. The techniques employed show many of the skills involved as well as some of the problems that can be encountered by the designer in translating the design into reality and on to film or tape.

WAREHOUSES
Commercial warehouses are sometimes used with or without some adaptation. BBC Bristol used this solution for the drama series *Casualty*, adding some basic facilities and providing successfully a permanent base for the programme over a long period of time.

Commercial warehouses can be rented easily and can provide an ideal covered working space for use by a television or film unit. From a design point of view they provide dry and clean space in which to set up a temporary props store and mini workshop, or perhaps as a main base from which to go out to shoot on other locations in the same area.

LOCATIONS
Working on location can call for the designer to provide many different levels of professional assistance to the director, ranging from a suggested shot or sequence of shots on a location that requires no scenic provision at all to a major construction build taking place in what ostensibly is a most unlikely location. The level of work is determined by the director and designer working through the script together. The range of design work that might be needed can be broken down as follows:

Interiors without any design work required
Occasionally some location interiors, by reason of their known existence or generic style, (for example railway stations, post offices, shops, garages, etc), may be used without having to provide any design treatment. However, as soon as there are

any specific requirements called for by the action or the dialogue, it is likely that the appearance of that particular location
will have to be modified even if minutely.

Interiors without any design work required, but matching other sequences

Often it is the case that although there is no work required on
the actual location itself, there may be a shot planned that
requires visually matching with a set being built on the film
stage or in the electronic studio. This means that the designer
has to plan carefully with the director how to achieve a convinc-
ing 'match' between the location and another sequence shot
elsewhere. This match might consist of building replica architectural features, but in any case requires carefully planned
camera shots, perhaps using some masking device (anything
from an actor to a specially-built wall or a parked vehicle) that
will convey to the audience the impression of one location
whether or not that is the case.

Interiors with design work required

Some location interiors may need some construction effort, but
in any case they will require decoration and prop dressing
without any specific visual link or relationship with previous or
subsequent shots. These are relatively straightforward tasks
for the designer, as they are clearly defined and do not depend
upon other decisions or factors.

Interiors with design work required and matching other sequences

If the designer has done the job well, interiors on location look
as if they have received virtually no design treatment at all and
that the unit simply had to walk in, rehearse and shoot the
action. What is often not realised is the amount of preparation
involved in achieving this appearance. Bearing in mind the
possibilities available by editing together a pre-planned sequence of shots, it does not always follow that the sequence
is in fact shot at one location. It could be that the imposing
exterior of a building is at one location, the entrance hall and
staircase at another and the upper floor reception rooms at a

third, because each separate element in the script calls for visual characteristics or physical requirements that simply cannot be found within one place. In this case, the designer has to plan carefully, matching links between different shots with dressing and continuity in order to convince the viewer that there is one location and not three.

Interiors within which to build other settings

It is sometimes the case that existing interiors are not simply altered but are used as quasi studio spaces in which the sets can be built. Although not an ideal solution, it is sometimes necessary and is a good example of how an evaluation of shooting in this way may provide the most cost effective answer.

Exterior locations

The main difference when working on exterior locations is the scale of the operation, travel and organisation and the weather. This involves not just rain, wind and light during the shoot itself, but in winter, the effect of frost on the drying qualities of paint and the setting properties of plaster or concrete. All these eventualities have to be planned for by having some interior scenes ready to be shot if weather is bad, in order to avoid expensive hold-ups. This type of planning may have knock-on effects as far as design costs are concerned, but has to be seen as being in the best financial interests of the production. Costs are usually agreed with the producer, director and production accountant on location at the time.

OUTSIDE EVENTS

Television outside events sometimes provide the need for design effort. On state occasions the designer might be called upon to build camera or vehicle hides that will 'fit in' visually to the architectural surroundings. As usual this entails planning camera shots so that the maximum effect can be gained by the cameras in the hides. However, when other cameras cannot avoid seeing the hides, their positions must be disguised as far as possible. Here the designer's skills at counterfeiting reality are put to a very real test. Similar work might be ncessary at classical music concerts, presentations, awards, and other civic or social ceremonies.

Outside broadcasts from theatres, the opera or the ballet occasionally call for some assistance from the television designer involving the adaptation from the relatively static visual image on the stage to television's multi-faceted images of the same subject. (Adapting productions from the theatre to television requires particular care. It may sometimes be necessary to have the stage designer working alongside the television designer in order to achieve the effect of the stage play on the television screen).

ROCK/POP/CHARITY CONCERTS

If involved in the televising of pop concerts, one of the main problems to be encountered by the television designer is that of unaccustomed scale. The viewing distances and size of wide shot can be so great as to require exceptional planning and visualisation, so that the design of the staging works as a spectacle in very long shot, still has relevance in the close, hand-held shots that will be taken on stage. It is an ideal scenario for the use of the CAD system which can predict very precisely the lens necessary to include the required image, or alternatively demonstrate what can and cannot be seen within the parameters of the building, space and equipment available.

Chapter 2

The Present Situation in
Television Production Design

The situation in television today is one of radical change which involves technological, social and political developments, endless visual possibilities and even gimmickry, as well as altered programme-making styles and perceptions. In the past, large organisations like the BBC made their programmes as part of a plan for the year, with a strong emphasis on pre-planning so that all programmes were completed on time and to the best possible quality. Although in some respects this is still the case, there is now a very different approach by some organisations, which derives from a financial pragmatism based more on quantitative than on qualitative judgements.

Directors and designers are faced with tighter budgets and shorter timescales within which to make productions and also with an almost bewildering choice of new visual treatments and techniques that are available at a price. There are many hard decisions to be made.

The programme makers
The designer in television is first and foremost a member of the programme-making team which brings to the screen a dramatic or comedy script, entertainment or musical score, or a programme idea from news, current affairs, documentaries or presentation. Obviously programmes vary enormously in size and content, length and number and, consequently, programme-making teams are composed differently according to the type of programme being made — examples are given later in the book of the main types to be met (see p.60). On major productions a large support team is drawn together and backs up the work of the various technical experts, whereas on smaller enterprises is it likely that one member of the team may cover several roles at once.

The production designer in television
There is an element of production design in nearly every programme seen on the screen today, from the most complex drama through to straight news reporting. It is difficult to say how much awareness of this fact exists among the television audience because so much of the designers' work can (and in

many cases arguably should) go unnoticed — except by their peers. The role of the production designer in television is to visualise the production in advance through a series of images, bearing in mind their accompanying sounds, to know the techniques involved and then to employ them, or enable others to employ them, during the process of the shoot or recording.

The designer's primary task is to provide an emotional visual response to the programme idea as a means of expressing and amplifying it and at the same time contributing an integral part of the production through the realisation of that response. In this way a visual programme style is evolved, (always in close conjunction with the other technicians working on the pro-gramme) that is in sympathy with the treatment proposed by the writer, director and producer. This style of visual interpre-tation and presentation is then carried out by the creative team under the overall guidance of the director.

What is production design in television?
When describing design, either as a verb or a noun, certain words and phrases tend to enter people's minds:

artistic idea	plan	realisation
preliminary	future product	achievement
intend	combination of details	
sketch	contrive	

In reducing this list my choice might look like this:

artistic idea	combination of details
plan	realisation and achievement

Reducing even further to the fundamentals of design, it can be said that the design process has two essential components:

- The artistic idea (the creation of the concept and artistic ideas).
- Its realisation (the translation of these ideas into the reality of a television production or programme.

Looking back over these descriptions and definitions it is obvious that the designer is involved with planning for the future, looking ahead and organising ideas of a visual and conceptual nature on a broad scale.

To achieve the best visual results for a programme, the designer should be involved from the earliest stage as an integral part of the production process, and not simply as a provider of scenic items in response to a pre-determined request by a director or producer. The unstated implication of this type of request is "don't worry yourself about the programme content because it need not concern you; stick to what you know about, namely design, and just supply the requested items without any further discussion". In the past some programmes did, and no doubt even now some programmes still do, get made in exactly that way, but they are likely to end up the poorer for rejecting ideas out of hand. A good designer's ideas, based on a visual response to the programme idea, are capable of contributing a much more imaginative overall statement that encapsulates and expresses better the programme intention and helps to achieve a far better presented end result.

Effective member of the production team
To be an effective member of the production team, the designer must acquire a thorough awareness of production methods and in particular the requirements and techniques of the other technical experts (lighting, sound, cameras, vision, recording, editing and video effects). The designer must also understand the other design disciplines (graphics, costume, scenic art, visual effects and make-up). The reason for this 'jack of all trades' approach is that, especially in the context of a studio recording, the designer's job is to work closely with the director in planning the production in order to contrive a floor plan that not only expresses the agreed design solution, but also enables all members of the team to achieve their own contributions.

Studio recordings
Studio recordings actually demand the creation of visual environments in which programmes can take place. The audience

THE SECRET AGENT

The following photographs illustrate graphically the complex problems to be faced in planning, setting up and shooting a drama, and indicate some of the techniques employed; these are much the same whether used on a lot, on a location or even on a film stage.

The first thing to note is the sheer scale of such an operation. If we look first at a typical shot called for by the script, it looks impressive in its evocation of period and atmosphere (see front cover), but gives no suggestion of the turmoil that is taking place behind the solid-looking walls. By looking a little to one side, the limits of the camera shot can be easily seen, defined in this case by the scaffolding structure and the office block and car park in the background.

The next thing to be aware of is the complexity of inter-related tasks that are being undertaken by the various craft teams within the overall production team, but more important the physical volume of items of equipment and materials that are necessary to all these experts if they are to carry out their appointed tasks.

It is easy when planning a location shoot, for the individual leaders of the respective teams (designer, lighting camera operator, costume designer, make-up and visual effects) to be concentrating solely (but naturally enough) on their own requirements, and to forget until they arrive on location how much space is needed — not only for their own equipment and services, but for everyone else's too. Hence the need for location managers to try to sort out the conflicting and competing demands for space and facilities.

The **lighting camera operator** and **electricians** have large and small lamps, cables, blocks, lamp stands, scaffold rigging, reflector boards, cameras and camera mountings and equipment, all of which has to be transported in a suitably sized lorry and be parked somewhere convenient on the site (but avoid getting into shot!).

Where **visual effects** are used, large amounts of materials and equipment are required to create the effects, e.g. rain, snow, smoke, pyrotechnics, and trick effects of all kinds. Again, the prime requisite is storage space and security and also working space for preparation.

The **design** requirements are firstly to make the scenic elements look right for the script and the camera shots, but also to consider the need for safe access for the artists and everyone constructing the set. The artists must be able to get to doors and windows when all the other work has been completed. Account must be taken of the physical needs of the production team, so that sets are strong enough to take the required load and, if possible, allow sufficient storage space.

The **production team** also provides its own set of facilities to help the smooth running of the shoot; these can involve hydraulic lift trucks for camera mountings, coaches and vehicles for transporting actors and the unit in general and, sometimes, location caterers.

The **craft team**, depending on the size of the production, is made up of carpenters and painters, possibly a scenic artist and a signwriter, often accompanied by scaffolders or steelworkers, plasterers occasionally drapes and other specialist contractors. Their tools and materials require adequate storage preferably protected from the weather.

The **prop team** need to have a suitable storage area to sort props and re-organise them for specific scenes during the shoot; sometimes this has to be the prop van itself.

is well aware of this fact and, as well as being conscious of the effort and imagination involved, accepts the idea that a designer has been called upon to conjure up the setting in which the production takes place. Studio recordings are not only recognisable, but bring with them expectations in the minds of the audience.

Location recording/shooting
The essence of a location shoot is the complex process of planning (and changing), matching (and changing), building (and changing), propping (and changing), improvising (and changing) in order to achieve a result that is visually appropriate for the (sometimes) hundreds of scenic locations and component parts of a programme idea. As well as originating everything necessary to make a particular location look right for the scene being shot, the results must look unobtrusive and natural when seen alongside those juxtaposed shots and sequences that have been shot with very little, if any, design treatment.

Ironically, it is in such circumstances that the audience and sometimes even critics ask what precisely the designer had done, making the assumption that, in some miraculous fashion, all the locations existed in exactly the right configuration to suit the action, camera shots, story and shooting schedule, and that all the production team had to do was to turn up and shoot. A television critic once suggested that a famous production designer "should have donated his fee to God", as he could not see what design work had been done on a prestigious location drama; needless to say the designer chose to keep his fee — and justifiably so.

Technical considerations
First the designer has to meet the demands of the script or idea in order that the actors or presenters are provided with an environment and visual style that enhances the storyline and their performances in an appropriate fashion. The next thing the designer has to do is to help meet the needs of the other members of the realisation team by enabling their contributions to take place in optimum conditions.

Budgets

Financially, the designer has a crucial role to play by designing not only to the programme brief but also within an agreed budget. This may sound like stating the obvious, but in practice life is seldom that simple, and can frequently lead to situations that are much less clear than would be the imaginary case simply stated on paper. This subject of budgeting and estimating costs will be dealt with at greater length in Chapter 5.

Chapter 3

The Context of Design

The design process described below is assumed to be for a studio-based comedy or drama production (despite the fact that the latter rarely occurs at the present time) and that there will be some location filming or video included in the final edit. This is because these types of programme use a wide range of studio resources and procedures and are convenient vehicles with which to examine the design contribution of the studio-based programme making process as it has developed up to now.

The differences presented by drama on location are generally referred to within the text, and elsewhere its implications for the designers of today and tomorrow are also discussed.

Smaller productions would obviously cut out many of the procedures described, as well as some of the staff referred to, as obviously more than one job would be carried out by one person.

The language of television
There is a common language used in the direction of television for the purpose of describing the many orders to be given and decisions to be made; it is a language that is understood the world over and can involve everyone in the production team.

Of prime importance to the designer are the language of camera shots, the language of camera moves and the language of vision mixing and linking shots; these three sets of terms go to describe the putting together of a series of specific shots in a manner that will be understood by everyone.

Working within the grammar of television
There are obviously many other terms used, for example in sound and lighting, recording, by floor managers and production managers and there are also some different terms used when working in film, but these will be easily picked up. The terms on p.43 give the basic elements of television language which are used to convey ideas to the director with speed and precision either in the planning stage or when shooting.

Camera shots: basic		Camera shots: additional	
Abbreviation	*Shot*	*Abbreviation*	*Shot*
CU	Close-up	BCU	Big close-up
MCU	Medium close-up		
MS	Mid shot		
MLS	Medium long-shot		
LS	Long shot	VLS	Very long shot
		WS	Wide Shot
		POV	Point of view

Camera moves

Pan	Pan right; pan left
Tilt	Tilt up; tilt down
Elevate	Go up
Depress	Go down
Track	Track in; track out
Crab	Crab left; crab right
Zoom	Zoom in; zoom out

Vision mixes

Cut	(Immediately between shots)
Mix	(Between shots at differing speeds)
Wipe	(Fast devices to transform screen from one image to another)
Overlay	
Super	(Superimpose)
Lose	(The super)
Insert	(Captions)
Fade up	
Fade out	
Fade sound and vision	

Close-up
CU

Medium close-up
MCU

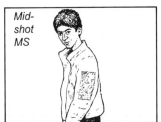

Mid-shot
MS

Medium long shot
MLS

Long shot
LS

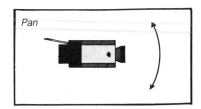

Pan

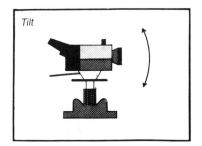

Tilt

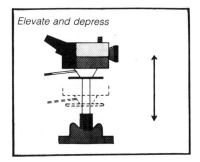

Elevate and depress

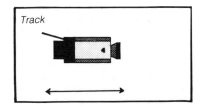

Track

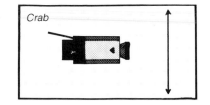

Crab

Shot sizes

Camera movements

The main categories of programme the designer works on

DRAMA

Drama productions make tremendous demands on the designer and at the same time they present, for many, the most satisfying challenge, and one to which nearly all young designers aspire. This challenge is not only to the designer as a creative contributor, but also to the designer as a fixer or achiever of the near impossible — someone who can retain in the mind's eye an original concept while carrying out the practical realisation under enormous pressure. Drama programmes can call for the designer to possess a strong sense of historical detail or just as keen an awareness of contemporary style and fashion.

Today, although so much television drama is made on location the demands are nevertheless as great as they have ever been. They call for the designer to be not only visually aware but to be creative, imaginative, well organised and able to carry a heavy workload while working to fast-changing deadlines that at times seem to be absolutely impossible. On film, for example, it might be necessary to plan the next day's unavoidably re-arranged shoot the previous evening, and have it ready for shooting early the next morning.

The designer also has to be more acutely aware than ever of the budget, (which can be extremely high on some major television productions, approaching the size of a small film) and always be conscious of alternative methods of effecting a particular design solution.

There are, in effect, three different types of drama productions.

DRAMA PLAYS

Drama plays tend to be looked upon by the television design community at large as the Rolls Royce vehicles of the programme fleet, and the ones on which all designers should aspire to work as the culmination of their careers. This theory is borne out by the film and television awards ceremonies that generally give their prizes to prestigious dramas rather than other types of programme. In the earlier days of television, single plays certainly were prestige productions and one thinks of *Armchair Theatre*, *The Wednesday Play*, and the similar generic titles that have followed these over the years.

Plays, from the first, commanded the biggest budgets and therefore were able to demand the best possible production teams in terms of creativity, imagination, originality and experience. Inevitably, as techniques grew more sophisticated, skills developed and frontiers were extended resulting in greater costs. The designer could be called upon to work in any conceptual style, in any historical period with the appropriate visual style, and was expected to know what could be achieved by employing differing techniques and processes so that credible alternative plans could be considered. Also, direct comparison was made between television programmes and the many films that could be seen on the same channel within a few moments of the television programme itself, and that argument then used to justify the additional expense.

The inevitable result of growing costs has been a gradual reduction over the years in the number of plays produced and designed for television. As referred to earlier, in 1984 there was a conscious decision by the BBC to move out of the studios on to location and film, which further reduced the remaining life span of the studio play.

DRAMA SERIES
Drama series have always been quite different from drama plays, the basic differences being the amount of available time and money devoted to them. They were always made in much shorter time spans and for much smaller budgets per episode per hour. The designer of a drama series is required to be fast thinking, decisive, perceptive, pragmatic to a degree and superbly optimistic. The general move on to location has made the designer's life even more hectic, with the need to find, dress and often modify locations within a very tight timescale and a limited budget. From a working point of view life can be less

than satisfactory, as sometimes the overall series production schedule dictates that the same production team and designer may not be able to work together continuously within say, a thirteen-part run. There is not, therefore, the same opportunity to develop such a good working relationship as on a play with its much longer run-up period.

DRAMA SERIALS

Serials fall somewhere between plays and series, in that they generally do not have the same level of budgeting as the single play or film, but on the other hand they do gather together a production team that stays together until the production is complete, so that good working relationships are possible, and quality programmes emerge as a result.

COMEDY

The sets for a situation comedy often need to be just as atmospheric, naturalistic and sensitively designed as for a 'serious' drama, although on a smaller scale of operation.

Whereas a drama production will run in length from fifty minutes up to two hours or more on occasions, the average length for a comedy is thirty minutes or twenty-five minutes' worth of story-telling time generally effected before a studio audience. This rules out the opportunity for a lingering establishing shot of the set with all the information that can convey, but also brings with it the particular need for a large number of close-ups (in order to capture the gag lines and the all-important reactions from the other actors).

Situation comedies call for less naturalistic sets, relying instead on a more stereotypical approach, but the need remains to convey atmosphere and information within the confines of a much shorter timescale. The designer's job in these circumstances is to try and convey atmosphere and a stylistic feel in a more panoramic style of design; panoramic in the sense of providing designed backgrounds to cover the camera movements across the front of an open set, or occasionally by using planned access through specific camera traps.

Audience rostra, cameras, booms and other technical equipment all take up a large proportion of the studio, thus reducing the space available to the designer for erecting sets.

In either case, the designer has to work within severely constrained limits of space, caused by cameras working for the most part across the mouths of the open sets, and with the additional constraint of an audience needing to see and hear what is happening in the studio, whilst occupying roughly half the available studio area. This is by no means easy to reconcile and presents a new set of problems to be solved. The physical limits of the typical medium-sized studio with audience facilities dictate that there may be three or even four sets erected in front of the audience, and individually these can be little more than five to seven metres wide as a maximum, no matter how large

"... the designer has to work within severely constrained limits of space caused by cameras working .... across the mouths of the open sets".

the suggested set is supposed to be. Designing a baronial entrance hall or dining room within the space of a terraced cottage can be tricky to say the least!

Other than this restriction of space for setting and shooting, the craft techniques used for designing comedy programmes are very much the same as for drama. The same concern for research, for architectural and prop detail, matching to location, for planning shots both on film and in the electronic studio and for authentic and realistic scenic finishes holds good whichever of the two types of programme is being designed.

The production team is also similar in structure to that used in drama, though more streamlined due to the shorter length and quicker turn-round of the programmes.

VARIETY

Variety, or light entertainment (LE) programmes are quite different. Whereas comedy programmes are put together in a manner that is similar to drama in terms of planning and predicting what is going to happen, variety or entertainment programmes by their nature often only occur by chance.

A star performer — a singer or dancer, perhaps — happens to be available between other commitments or may be passing through London. Suddenly there is an opportunity to make a programme or even series, but only within what might in other circumstances be called impossible deadlines. This brings acute pressure to bear on the designer and with it the need to be ingenious by trying to design a set that may have to meet the needs of more than one star performer. Drawing dates and construction times stop for no-one, because in the end there is a physical limit on the amount of work that can be carried out by a construction workshop within a finite period. In this area of late starts and enforced late scripts and information, the designer has to be ready to achieve the impossible with a smile.

The LE designer needs to possess a strong feeling for the contemporary styling that is prevalent among the performers themselves. This might include the advertising images currently in vogue, TV commercials, magazines, the pop scene, dance, clothes and fashion as well as video promo tapes. The designer has to be just as well organised and pre-planned as for drama — especially as timescales are not only tighter but more likely to be based on less information.

The planning and conceptualising of an entertainment set takes a different form from drama by being involved with elements such as dance and a choreographer, music and a musical director, different staging techniques, different lighting and recording techniques and, nearly always, an audience.

The designer needs to be adaptable and quick witted in responding to a complex array of production requirements involving requests from all or any of the above people, but more important, needs to be able to create an atmosphere that becomes crucially important, especially in the case of a new series or with an artist who is, for instance, hosting their own show for the first time. In some respects it could be argued that to design this is more difficult than a drama set where there is usually far more information available, either from the writer, the script or from research material.

CHILDREN'S
Children's programmes have their own distinct characteristics and call for different design approaches.

In television, children's programmes usually have fairly restricted budgets, yet often have to broadcast each weekday for long periods of time. These two factors mean that the customary design solutions which would work for, say, a comedy or entertainment programme suddenly become not only impossible, but more important, inappropriate. Children's programmes call for a simple, direct yet very economic design approach that will complement the producer's ideas for a series directed at a particular age or interest group.

Ironically, at a time when experience and accumulated skills are arguably needed most, producers of programmes for children working in larger organisations may find they have been allocated some of the least experienced designers. The plus side of this equation is that newer and younger designers may bring a freshness of style, great enthusiasm and a willingness to put considerable efforts into the programme to make sure their design is a success.

MUSIC
Music programmes used to be made in television studios during the '60s and '70s, but this is now seldom the case. In years gone by, studio recorded programmes would include operas such as *Billy Budd*, *Peter Grimes*, *Cosi fan Tutte* and

Michael Tippett's *New Year.* There were also programmes such as *Music for You, In Concert* and other recitals.

The trend in music programmes now is to relay or record live events from outside venues rather than use electronic studios.This change of habit has had a direct effect on design opportunities and undeniably reduced the scope of designers working on television's musical canvas.

The challenge of designing opera for television combines the demands of drama at its best, and then adds the requirements of music recording, perhaps of relaying sound from one studio to another and of using scenic, visual and or video effects to produce what is perhaps the most complex type of audio visual programme imagery to be seen on the TV screen.

DOCUMENTARIES
Documentaries involve design input only occasionally, and when they do can often bring with them intriguing problems for the designer to solve and for the producer to grapple with. The definition of documentary itself is a matter for some debate, but was described by the BBC back in 1972 as being a programme that explores a factual subject in depth, that illuminates and does not merely inform, but provokes deeper thought and understanding than a cold presentation of facts.

- It usually presents its subject at first hand (e.g. by use of film cameras on location) rather than at second hand (e.g. by discussion in a studio).

- It is a creative work — sometimes of the producer/director, sometimes shared between a producer and director, or between a producer/director and writer, or sometimes a writer.

- It varies in length and subject matter, can deal with history, the present day or speculate about future developments. It can confine itself to undisputed facts or it may be concerned with opinion.

- *It does not, however, normally make use of fiction.*

The sentence above is interesting in the context of design, because although a producer can, without departing from a responsibility to the subject matter, set out to entertain or to move, it is generally accepted as legitimate to use the skills of the film-maker, and *even the dramatist* in presenting the material. Both sets of italics are mine, as the interesting question that arises seems to be whether or not any use of a designer can be justified within the terms of the definition of the word documentary itself.

How far is it permissible to use the skills of the dramatist (and designer) to present facts or opinion and, in so doing, how far is it permissible to suggest people, places and objects rather than use the actual items themselves, because it could be argued that the use of drama (and design) within the documentary context is a fiction in itself and therefore a contradiction?

PRESENTATION

Although presentation studios are generally very small, they are very important to the general image of a broadcasting station, as they present to the viewer the most immediate visual identification of the company in the process of linking and trailing the programme schedule. Designers working in presentation face one of the most difficult challenges they are likely to come across, as the basic ingredient of TV design is missing — space. When there is an acute shortage of floor space (and ceiling heights that are far too low) there is always likely to be problems that make the basic expectation of a well- designed and well-lit picture extremely difficult to achieve. Nevertheless, it becomes a fascinating challenge for the designer.

In presentation work, it is crucial for the designer to establish a close working relationship with the graphic artist who is working in the presentation area, so that their work can be related and co-ordinated to realise the best results for the programme or the trailer or the links. Often on smaller stations and sites these two design areas overlap and there will be one designer to carry out both functions; this is particularly the case where CAD and DVE are available.

CURRENT AFFAIRS

When working on current affairs programmes the designer is immediately aware of the different structure of the production team — for a programme editor, producers who direct themselves and others who have assistant producers directing for them, research assistants who may direct some sequences, as well as directors of the day who are concerned primarily with making the studio work efficiently, rather than with editorial content.

This multiplicity of working arrangements reflects the need for flexibility and fluidity of treatment as the programme idea develops and changes with the discovery of new information that is relevant to the subject matter. Programme ideas are likely to be developing and changing up to the last minute, but there is still the need for a running programme to have its own clear and permanent identity, part of which is the studio setting where it regularly takes place.

When the designer first meets the programme editor or executive editor of individual current affairs programmes to discuss the subject treatment, it may not exist in anything more than an embryonic state. Nevertheless the designer must try to obtain a skeletal brief of the programme content, plus basic operational information concerning studio or location, cameras, sound facilities, length of recording, studio day(s), preparation time and budget.

Programme needs can range from a presenter with one interviewee (1+1), through the presenter with two opposing experts (1+2), to the presenter with three or four interviewees of differing views (1+3 & 1+4). Then there is the interview between the presenter and someone who may be many miles away, but who appears on a screen in the studio, perhaps to be in conversation with another person in the studio. In all these situations it is most important to be able to achieve shots of the presenter and guests in different combinations (single, matching singles, two shot, group shot, over shoulder shots and so on); they all require careful planning, especially when relating to pieces of furniture or scenery which can be difficult to change radically at the last moment.

The range of design treatment is wide in current affairs programmes, as it can include chat shows which are usually more akin to light entertainment in feel and atmosphere, political commentary and individual treatments of topical subjects. Whichever it is, the setting has to work on a 'feels right' basis, depending on whether the programme is serious, funny, interesting or arresting, and whether it is a new venture, a regular spot on the dial or a one-off 'special'. In these circumstances, with a different kind of production team and different methods of working, it is important for the designer to establish at an early stage the point of reference for decisions to be made.

Freedom of editorial choice is key to current affairs programmes and occasionally it may mean jettisoning a planned item that has already been realised in design terms (scenery built and props obtained), in favour of a last minute item that is of greater relevance. Although this goes against the grain for designers, it is an inevitable part of topical programme making and on occasions cannot be avoided. However, good planning and constant contact with the decision maker can usually avoid this problem.

On current affairs programmes, it is very important for the designer to work particularly closely with the graphic designer, especially on one-off programmes where the relationship between the graphic title sequences and programme content, and the scenic element of the programme is of vital importance for conveying a coherent production message.

Also, due to the intrinsic developing nature of such programmes, it is important for the designer to be involved to the extent of listening to the comments and opinions of the programme makers and to follow their train of thought as the programme idea and treatment emerges. If that is the case, there will be a far better chance of the designer being able to reflect this appropriately in the setting or studio environment.

For all these reasons, pilots and rehearsal time are used a great deal in current affairs so that by the time a topical, and very often live, programme is broadcast the editorial, technical and visual problems will have been largely resolved, leaving the subject matter to speak for itself in the best possible circumstances.

NEWS

An interesting challenge facing the designer of a news studio or the presentation of a regular news programme is that like re-designing the layout of a national newspaper, a change of setting for television news tends not to happen very often, and therefore the opportunity to gain such experience is rare. This is because the decision to change the style of an organisation's news output invariably comes from the highest editorial level and represents a change in programme and corporate policy. The realisation of this policy change involves detailed and critically important planning by the designer, as the margins for error are absolutely minute and, once made, cannot be easily disguised by the conventional means of prop dressing or changing the camera shot.

Consequently, when a change of policy and news output does occur enormous interest is generated and many members of the team wish to have an input into the design process. So, instead of having to deal with one or perhaps two people (as in the case of director and producer in other programme areas), the designer can end up in meetings with the full team, all of whom have a vested interest in the design from their respective positions and interests. An initial meeting might include the editor, together with newsreaders, journalists, producers, assistant producers, the graphic designer, music composer, lighting director, sound and engineering staff. From then on, the problem is one of recognising what is the desired solution and trying to realise it while discussions may be still continuing. As with current affairs, it is often necessary for the designer to establish exactly who is the decision maker within this collection of enthusiastic programme makers, so problems can be referred for a speedy response.

More than in any other environment in television, an assessment of the ergonomic implications is crucial within the context of newsreaders' desks and chairs, including as they often do built-in monitors, computers, microphones, telephones and video screens, not to mention sheets of paper and writing facilities. Not only must the equipment fit the individual working with it, but the camera shots must be attainable, as there is so little margin for error and very little can be done to correct matters if the initial planning goes awry.

It is an area in which mock-up prototypes are not just invaluable but are essential, as is the need to have all equipment built into the desk and scenery at the contractor's workshop to ensure accurate fitting and safe working.

The successful design of the best news programmes might be described as 'simple but interesting' — and involve much commonsense in approach. The designer has to recognise and reflect visually the editorial initiative that has brought about the need for change in the presentation of the news and the design of the news studio and try to express on the screen the new editorial image sought. A number of questions need to be posed, for example:

- How many presenters are envisaged; one or two?
- Are they of equal importance or is one senior to the other?
- How is this recognised in the shots that are planned?
- Will the presenters be interviewing during the bulletin?
- If so, how many people are involved and how many at one time?
- What elements of the old-style news were successful and will be retained?
- What elements of the old-style news need to be jettisoned and replaced?
- What technical facilities are required, and how do they impinge on the design?

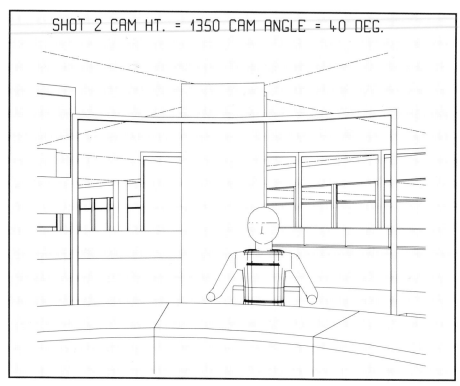

SHOT 2 CAM HT. = 1350 CAM ANGLE = 40 DEG.

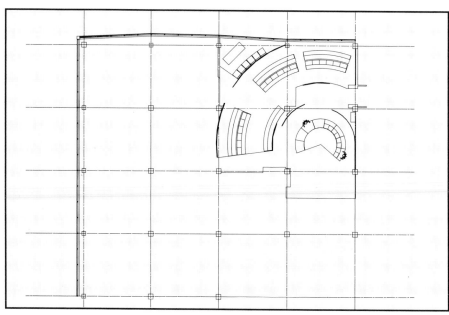

The image of the newsreader in the context of a newsroom was achieved with the help of computer aided design; a 3D model was created in the computer, which then predicted the camera shot and allowed any alterations to be made at the planning stage, prior to the construction process.

Often news studios have limited space, so the precise and careful planning of the operation of that studio is vital in an environment that is used as a 'workspace that is to be seen' several times each day. Access is all important as is the provision of fire exits and fire lanes; if there is one cardinal rule in these circumstances it must be to keep the presenter as far away from the backing as space allows. Adequate spacing between the newsreader and the backing is the one element in the design and lighting of a news studio that is of the utmost importance if a well balanced and appropriately atmospheric picture is to be obtained.

The aimed-for 'simple but interesting' visual approach can create a deceptively false impression that a news studio is a simple design problem to solve. Nothing could be further from the truth and the complexity and exacting demands of this type of work should never be under-estimated; they require every bit as much creativity and attention to detail as does a major drama, although in a very different mode.

OUTSIDE BROADCAST EVENTS

The designer is seldom called upon to assist with outside events, but these can occasionally present intriguing problems, such as the need to build camera hides that do just that but are in the style of Wren, or merging OB scanner vans into the landscape at Windsor Castle (see p.41). This work is more in the nature of a camouflage exercise, but one that is subject to the scrutiny of the television camera and close-up lens. It calls for all the craft skills available to achieve a satisfactory and unobtrusive result that allows a major state occasion to be televised whilst drawing the least amount of attention to the means by which the programme is made.

Broad groupings of programmes

Seen from a purely design viewpoint, television programmes can be gathered together into broad categories based on the accrued experience of many designers over the years and the production requirements that tend to emerge with some regularity from certain programmes. These are obviously not hard and fast categories and are not intended to be anything more than a convenient vehicle on which to explore the different approaches adopted by designers in their work on television programmes. The categories would consist of the following groups:

- Drama and comedy
- Variety, children's and music
- News, presentation, current affairs and documentaries.

Composition of the different production teams

Although we have seen that there is a basic language used throughout television, the composition of production teams differs according to the traditions behind the particular type of programme being made, the organisation or company making it, and the person who in the end is responsible for the total project.

Full-scale drama productions, by reason of their size, complexity and the consequent cost of the resources involved, can be expected to carry the most comprehensive production teams. The producer and director are the two key individuals in the team. The producer is normally the person who launches a project and has overall creative responsibility (sometimes working to an executive producer who has responsibility for several projects at once). The director is usually the person in charge of the performance of the artists, cameras and the entire production and realisation team (often working with the help of 1st and 2nd assistants and usually with a production manager). They are supported by others such as script editor, associate producer, production accountant, location manager, AFM (assistant floor manager), floor assistant, production assistant and production secretary.

In variety and comedy, producers traditionally direct and in journalistic programmes (including documentaries, news and current affairs) an editor takes the role of the producer, producers and assistant producers direct and also directors are often brought in to operate the studio on the day, with researchers directing parts of programmes or simple sequences.

All these functions vary slightly within each organisation and production and, increasingly, there are production management companies springing up whose job it is to provide the organisational infrastructure necessary to mount an individual production or series where the originator of the idea does not wish to assume that responsibility. The composition of the design team will also vary according to circumstance and demand. If a production designer is heading the team, there will probably be an art director(s), assistant art director(s) and/or design assistant(s), a construction manager, production buyer, property master and the support crews necessary to undertake the work in hand.

Other programmes

The design team outlined above is an example of the large-scale design team on a major drama. Assuming the same level of demand for resources, the same team would be used to service a production from any other programme area. As the demand for resources is reduced so the design team changes and reduces until on a very small production there may be a designer who arranges everything and is assisted by no-one.

Chapter 4

The Design Process

With such a wide variety of programmes, being designed by many different designers of differing experience and backgrounds, working with directors of equally different experience, there is inevitably considerable variation in the methods employed in designing for television. Despite these differences, certain basic essentials remain constant within the design and realisation process in almost every programme-making context; the designer joins the programme, is given information by the director on which is based the creative design process. Then, the design has to be realised either in a studio or on location and within an agreed budget.

How, why and when a designer arrives

Different types of programme call for different design skills, different approaches and differing sympathies from the designer, so it is obviously of the utmost importance for the producer and director to acquire the designer who they think will best meet the particular needs. In large design departments, a belief usually exists that designers should, where possible, design a wide range of productions in the interests of career development, as many of the lessons learned in one programme area can easily provide the trigger mechanism for an inspired approach when applied to a design problem in totally different area of programme making.

Producers, on the other hand, would naturally argue for the use of the specialist designer — one who regularly works with the same director on the same type of programme. They provide strong reasons for doing so and question who should decide about the allocation of designers to programmes. Which is more important, the producer's and director's choice of designer on a particular programme or the offer of an alternative choice in the interests of the organisation itself and the all-round future development of the designer as a professional practitioner?

In the freelance world many partnerships between producers/-directors and designers have been established and often have survived for a period of years on the basis of invitations which materialised as a result of a successful last job. So, however much this idea of career development might be pursued as policy by managers and designers in a design department, in the freelance world the problem does not actually exist, because the producer's choice is the decisive element in the end, whether operating from personal knowledge or through an agent. This policy has been introduced recently in the BBC throughout the programme-making process, giving full responsibility to the individual producer to choose the right team.

RESEARCH

When to research a production is very much a matter for debate. In a sense the designer needs to read the script first in order to obtain those all-important first impressions on which the design of the production is built, but it is also true that some useful background research can illuminate the first reading and give greater significance and an added dimension to the script. Quite often the designer and producer both know that a production is to take place some months later, so the intervening period may provide an ideal opportunity for research before becoming involved with the actual script in its final form.

Read the book

Sometimes the script is adapted from a book or from another play, or even from a film or video; a libretto may have been adapted from a play. It may be useful to read such material and any other relevant work such as critical reviews.

Explore around the subject

Design research is a subject in itself and a considerable amount of time and space could be devoted to it; suffice to say that within the confines of time and resources allowed for the making of television programmes, the main sources of information for the acquisition of quick answers to reference questions are to be found in several main areas. Encyclopaedias (particularly illustrated versions), portraits (particularly for the information contained in the backgrounds of the pictures), country houses, paintings in general — even those of little artistic value in themselves — can provide invaluable historical detail. Dictionaries are all-important — the full editions will be necessary rather than shorter or concise ones — specialist periodicals, catalogues, advertisements, picture sources (photographic collections in particular, and of course museums, not to mention foreign institutes, libraries and embassies), all provide possible sources of visual information. The designer (with a design researcher if the production is rich enough to have one) will want to gather together as much background information and research as there is time for, in order to be well informed about the locale, period, place, social customs and history of the particular programme idea.

Carry out visual research

Visual research plays a vital role in the initial discussions between the director and designer. Producing a reproduction, whether it is a postcard, in an art book or cut from a newspaper supplement is for both the director and the designer a clear indication of the way in which they are respectively seeing the stylistic direction in which they think a play could go. The names of painters or periods or styles or films or even other TV programmes can all be indicators of the way in which the designer or the director is thinking, and of images that seem to be appropriate to their vision of the script.

Some directors have been known to set up their offices with an abundance of visual reference so that all the various participants in the creative team can have common visual points of reference from which to start their discussions. At the initial stage, the director is likely to be more concerned with the storyline and the verbal interpretation of the script and have a less clearly developed idea of the visual composition of the piece as a whole.

Searching for a visual style for the programme is one of the most exciting and absorbing parts of the designer's and director's working relationship. It develops over the initial period of the production as information is gathered, ideas are generated, evaluated and sometimes discarded, until a point is reached at which the production style can be seen to be firming up as a working guideline to the realisation of the programme.

Co-ordinating research
At the same time as the designer is researching, the chances are that other members of the production team are doing exactly the same thing; the director with the AFM may well be researching into performance, as in the case of a period play or opera, or simply into social customs and human behaviour as they are likely to affect the actors' performance. Also the costume and make-up designers will be researching, as will the lighting director and the graphic designer.

Quite often these areas of research can be useful to the designer in the continuing search for background and visual information; equally, the research carried out by the design team can be of great value to the director and actors, as well as other colleagues on the production team. It is very worth-while cross referring with the other team researchers not only to avoid duplication, but also to alert everyone to the information that is available. On some major productions, professional researchers are employed to obtain such information and they can co-ordinate research to a large extent across the whole team, as well as provide a fund of visual and literary sources.

BREAKING DOWN THE SCRIPT
The process involved in breaking down a drama script, is key to the whole process of television design, as it typifies the attention to detail required to realise successfully a creative and imaginative design concept. There is a saying among television designers that the creative part of the job takes about 5% of the time, but the realisation of that concept takes up the remaining 95% and is sheer hard slog.

FIRST IMPRESSIONS
When looking at a script initially, it is a good idea to read it simply as a storyline and at the same time be aware of the many

first impressions that will inevitably come from that first contact, and to note them down so that they are not lost. First impressions are very precious to the creative designer, and often, though by no means always, turn out to be the ones that finally carry weight as the design develops through its various stages. They can take many forms involving visual composition, concepts for key shots, the mood and atmosphere for specific settings, colour, sound, music, effects, in fact all or any of the elements that will contribute to the realisation of the concept and interpretation of the script and story.

Because there are so many influences at work on the designer at this early stage, and so many things to remember when developing design ideas, this process can be broken down into some of its main elements and each one looked at separately. This is, of course, not intended to suggest that this particular method of approach is superior to any other. What is important is that the designer is aware of these elements in the early stages of a production and, in their own way, incorporates the effect into the final design proposal.

Understanding the story
At the risk of stating the obvious, it is crucial that a clear understanding of the storyline is gained at the earliest possible stage. Of vital importance is the asking of any questions that arise in the designer's mind from that first reading of the script. It is quite possible that some contributory fact may have been overlooked during the initial read, but on the other hand it could indicate that some point in the story is not totally clear or may need emphasis. Whatever the reason, it can only be clarified by discussion with the director, who in turn may wish to consult the writer. So, the designer should note down these first impressions and questions so that they can be brought up during the first design meeting with the director.

Emotional response
The designer's emotional response to the story is a good indicator of thought patterns and can provide corroboration that director and designer are on the same creative wavelength

from the earliest stages of the production. At the first design meeting, the answer to the director's question "Well, what did you think of the script then?" gives the designer the opportunity to express something of an instinctive reaction to the story and its treatment by the writer. Although they will often be strong enough to remain clearly in focus without recourse to pencil and paper, it may be worth noting down some of these thoughts; the important thing is that they are nurtured while in their embryonic stage and not forgotten.

Initial visual impressions and opportunities

While reading through the script, the designer will inevitably be struck by initial visual impressions and opportunities that come off the page as the story unfolds. Sometimes these are specified by the writer as integral elements in the story and could take the form of specific shots of artists, sets, props or effects, but at other times the stage directions deliberately invite a greater freedom of expression for the director and designer to suggest their own visual means by which the story can be most effectively progressed.

The designer will quickly recognise a pattern emerging from the initial visual impressions suggested by the story and script. This creates opportunities to amplify the story by relating these visual impressions to the developing design concept. These first impressions are usually noted down in the script alongside the stage directions and the dialogue concerned and can take the form of sketches, storyboard jottings or notes as necessary.

Underlying dramatic and visual structure

In the theatre, design is concerned with the relationship between the actor and space and the resulting three-dimensional form of a performance that is presented direct to the audience, each of whom sees the action from a slightly different viewpoint. The most appropriate form of expression to convey the concept is by a 3-D model, supported by sketches.

In television, design is concerned with two-dimensional images which are seen by the audience on a video screen. Every member of the audience sees an image of the action from an identical viewpoint (the camera) that takes place in a (designed) three-dimensional environment, but nevertheless the end result is two-dimensional images on the screen; therefore the most appropriate form of expression to convey the concept is by two-dimensional means supported by models. Two-dimensional sketches vary according to the individual designer, but can be pencil drawings, atmospheric sketches and paintings. Video recordings of planned shots, location recces, models or effects can also be made by the designer and manipulated with a digital paint system.

Storyboard jottings

Camera shots obviously have to be carefully considered and planned for by the designer, not only as individual key shots but also as sequential shots. This concern with the planning of sequences of shots involves other members of the realisation team (e.g. director, camera, lighting, sound, costume, etc.) and are usually sketched by the designer in the form of a storyboard, i.e. a sequence of camera shots fully described in order to achieve the desired effect (see p.71).

Storyboards vary enormously in their treatment and the amount of time spent on them, which depends on the draughting skills of the particular designer, the time available and the nature of the sequence. They can either be in the form of conceptual sketches with accompanying notes for camera, lighting and sound, etc, or in the case of pre-planned digital video effects or special effects, with accompanying plans and diagrams to indicate how the particular effect (with all its integral parts) is intended to be realised and by whom.

Therefore, when reading through the script for the first time, the designer will recognise that certain parts of the story need to be planned as a sequence of shots in order to express them creatively. So storyboard jottings of the broad intention of the sequence will be made in the script, so that they can be developed further at a later stage, when more discussions have taken place and additional information is available.

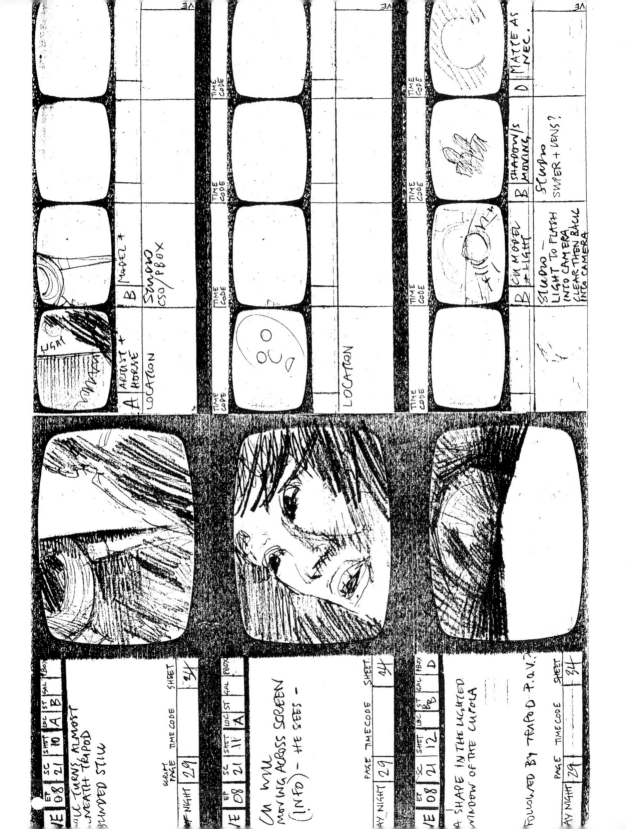

Unusual problems and/or effects

It is also wise in the first read-through of the script to extract immediately those problems which are recognised as unusually large, require difficult and expensive effects or will obviously have a major effect on the planning of the production schedule and budget. More often than not, these items will have been allowed for in the initial production budget, but the debate then needs to be taken further with the relevant members of the team to establish whether the allowance is sufficient in terms both of the time taken to set up and achieve the effect, as well as the actual cost of building or preparing it.

Questions to be answered

At the end of the first reading of the script, it is always a good idea to gather together any other unanswered questions that might have arisen. Many outstanding points will be answered during the next stages of the design process, but a daily checklist procedure of 'Jobs in hand — Jobs to do — Jobs to be started' is one that most designers carry out in some fashion or another.

SECOND IMPRESSIONS

Having read the script through for the first time, the designer is left with many different sensations and a great sense of anticipation. There is the excitement of a new project, perhaps of working with new colleagues, and the opportunity to make a creative contribution to a complex production.

There are also a significant number of unanswered questions arising out of the first impression of the story which invite further investigation, many of which will yield their answers in response to closer examination of the script. So the next thing to do is precisely that — to read the script through again, but this time with a different purpose in mind. Having deliberately concentrated upon the visual, emotional and dramatic impressions in the first reading, the designer now concentrates more on the finer points of detail making sure that none of the key textual or visual information has been missed.

Study stage directions

The first place for the designer to study is the stage directions — the parts of the script traditionally typed in capital letters, usually at the beginning of a scene, but otherwise wherever the action or script demands. It is here that the writer tells the production team what is intended in terms of settings, action, layout of set or location, information about characters, quality of lighting, sound or special effects — in fact anything that is necessary to realise that part of the production more effectively.

This study requires a systematic and thorough scouring of the stage directions in order to extract the specifically design-orientated instructions first, then to note them for other members of the team, such as lighting, and extract or extrapolate from *their* instructions what are the implications for the designer. It is worth looking at this process in a little more detail to see the different elements involved.

For example, a subtle and changing lighting effect outside a studio window might well mean that painted and/or plain gauzes are needed, but most important it immediately suggests that the one essential element required is *space*; space in which to light, space to create depth, space in which to hang the gauzes and cloths. A knowledge of the principles of lighting will straightaway indicate the nature of the problem for the lighting director. The designer can at the early stage ensure that sufficient space is provided to co-ordinate their respective efforts to the greatest effect.

Study dialogue

Studying the dialogue can be very fruitful as an indicator of character information. Observing how characters speak, voice their opinions and thoughts, with information about their ages, health, family history, likes and dislikes, social contacts and whereabouts, occupation and recreation, these can all help the designer fill in the visual background. Such details can help the designer decide how best to make a set reflect a character with his or her past and present possessions and baggage — and sometimes even to convey a point of information in the script in purely visual rather than spoken terms. Sometimes the writer will provide design information in the dialogue that is not specifically referred to in the stage directions. The designer needs to be alert to all such references and be able to reflect them in the proposed design and thus present to the viewer as complete a picture as possible in the telling of the story. Out of this process should emerge a far clearer picture both of the characters themselves and the sets or environments in which they live or are found in the story.

Number and descriptions of sets and characters

Usually there is a breakdown of sets or locations noted on the script, and sometimes there is a basic running order or the limit and dates of a shooting schedule. This gives the up-to-date information regarding simple facts, but is no more than a starting point for the designer when breaking down the script. It is nevertheless a very useful starting point, as it allows quick early comparisons and feasibility studies to be made as the design proposals develop.

What concerns the designer in the early stage of a production is the relationship between the different characters and their sets; which sets or locations relate directly to a particular character or characters, and what are they able to tell the viewer about them? The style of building of the set, its careful dressing and choice of props can add vital information both about a character and also something of the background to the story in order to help advance it a little further. To do this there must be a conscious awareness of the whole script and its characters.

In practical terms, this will mean listing all the sets or locations known in simple terms, noting the number of scenes in each set, the length of these scenes and the characters in each scene in each set. It is then necessary to evaluate the dramatic significance of each scene regardless of length or the number of characters involved. It can often be the case that a dramatically vital scene which is of great importance to the story will take place in a familiar set, but on occasions the opposite is

Set List: taken from script breakdown

1. RECEPTION ROOM AND CORRIDOR INT/EXT.
2. HALL AND LANDING INT.
3. FRONT DOOR EXT.
4. GARAGE, STABLES & GARDEN EXT.
5. COUNTRY LANE WITH 'PHONE BOX EXT.
6. RAILWAY STATION EXT.

Set List: typical breakdown into scenes, with relevant stage directions

set name	pages	characters	year/time/season of day	scenic/prop re-setting/dressing	special requirements	special props
RECEPTION ROOM AND CORRIDOR						
scene 4 A	6-10	HENRY, SUE CHILDREN & PARENTS	1936 SPRING AFTERNOON	—	REAL DAFFODILS ON TABLE	OLD PIANO
scene 4 B	11-16	HENRY CHILDREN & PARENTS	SAME YEAR AUTUMN MORNING	ROOM RE-DECORATED SOME FURNITURE CHANGED	6 MONTHS LATER	FULLY PRAC RAIN O/S WINDOW.

true, namely that there is only the one vitally important scene in a particular set. When this happens there is an instant cost implication against which to compare its dramatic value, that is the expense of building and dressing the set for such a limited use. In such circumstances it is important to identify this possible anomaly and to establish a clear agreement with the director to support such a priority from the beginning of the realisation process.

The next layer of information to be extracted from the script is that concerning passage of time associated with the different sets or locations. What is of great importance here are the different lighting conditions called for, e.g. night and day, time of year, winter/summer, with their associated atmosphere. The suggestion of different types of light sources, e.g. candle, oil, gas, electric, adds the dimension of historical period to the realisation process. Within these parameters, there is the passage of time and the continuity element which can involve the designer in considerable re-dressing of props and even of re-building whole sets. For example, in order to convey the passage of a few months, one alternative would be for the set to be re-decorated or, alternatively, to convey the passage of a few years, for the set to age while retaining the same furnishings and layout. Whichever is the case, the designer has to decide how to achieve this change, how long it will take to effect in real time within the recording or shooting schedule and to decide with the production team when to schedule the change to avoid wasting the time of the whole unit.

Therefore, this will mean annotating the set list to take account of all these requirements.

Layout of key sets and props
Considering the relationship between sets and characters naturally leads on to the examination of the action that is to take place within those sets or locations. There will be certain requirements called for by the script. The main ones will certainly be noted in the stage directions; obvious examples are the specifying of entrances and exits, doors and windows or con-

necting spaces and the key props that go with them. These might be pieces of furniture, machines, horses and carriages, cars, bicycles, human feet walking, or simply action props used by the artists in the course of the scene.

A careful study by the designer of each set and those sets or locations adjacent to it either in geography or juxtaposition in the script, will reveal initial ideas for the layout of key props together with the principal moves of the actors. This leads on to an examination of the dramatic action and the main moves called for in the script, together with key shots, key sequences and key effects involved in those scenes. What must be checked is that the relationship between the different scenes works, in terms of editing together, of physical proximity in the studio and of being able to shoot them in the appropriate order when out on location.

Also at this stage the designer should recognise the need for changes that will assuredly come during the rehearsal period, as the director and actors develop their work together.

Identifying action and dressing props
This is the time to look again at the script, particularly the dialogue and stage directions to pick out all the action and dressing props required. The distinction between action and dressing props is one which has many different definitions, but for our purposes they can be distinguished as follows:

- **Dressing props** (see p.116): include *furniture* (sometimes called stage props) — chairs, tables, beds, sofas, bookcases, etc. Also **small props** — pictures and paintings, mirrors, vases, telephones, greenery.

- **Action props** (see p.116/118/119)): include actors' personal props e.g. wallet, glasses, money, etc, and also **hand props** — those items used in the action, such as a cup and saucer, book, pen; in fact anything that the actor uses in the plot.

It is sensible for the designer to work closely with the AFM (assistant floor manager) and properties buyer (or production buyer) when drawing up the lists of action and dressing props in order to avoid unnecessary duplication, but more important is to establish that the action props are carefully chosen to fit into the set and are correct in terms of period, colour, age and dramatic impact in the context of the action.

The other area of props supply that requires close liaison between designer, AFM and buyer are **special** props — that is those that are likely from the beginning to have to be specially acquired or made— and also whether and to what degree these and the other props are required to be **practical.** The designation practical denotes that a particular prop either (a) works completely — termed **fully practical**; (b) appears to work but in fact works only to a limited degree, termed **practical;** (c) is simply a piece of set dressing used as an incidental feature, termed **non-practical** — for example, a telephone, refrigerator, cooker, washbasin, bath, light fitting that appears in a set but is not used in any way.

Summarising the script requirements

Having read the script once and then appraised it a second time in more detail, it should be possible to summarise the production requirements, comparing them with the initial set breakdown and in so doing arrive at the first overview of the design requirements. This gives the designer a number of questions that lead into the design proposals to be presented shortly to the director.

Summarising design requirements

The first task is to evaluate the set list, considering questions such as these:

- Which sets contain the greatest number of scenes?
- What does this mean in terms of dramatic significance?
- What does this mean in terms of attention to detail?

- What does this mean in terms of treatment and cost?
- Which sets contain the least number of scenes?
- Could they be set in another set?
- Could they be set elsewhere?
- What is the writer's intention?
- What is the visual significance of the sets in relation to the story?
- Are they visually and dramatically so important as to justify themselves despite being used so little?

From evaluation of these questions, the designer will be able to decide upon priorities of time, effort, resources and money relative to the production value accorded to each item or section. At this point other factors need to be brought into play.

CONSIDER THE STYLE OF THE SCRIPT

What does the script call for in stylistic terms, both of performance and visual presentation? For a moment consider this *regardless* of cost. It is important not to be constrained by financial limits at too early a stage in the design process; the instant rejection of design proposals on cost grounds alone without exploring the possibility of re-jigging the design budget in .order to accommodate a really stunning idea can lead to financially secure but visually uninspired solutions. If the idea is 'right' in stylistic terms, then energies should be expended to ensure that it can be incorporated into the overall design concept within the budget by making adjustments elsewhere.

Another danger for the designer to guard against is the temptation to apportion money and resources based purely upon the statistical breakdown and divide a given budget accordingly. In fact the style of the writing, performance and visual presentation may well not call for locations or sets that are either as elaborate or expensive as a simple statistical division of the budget might imply, and the design style to be striven for could actually be far simpler and cheaper than the figures might suggest. The designer must be aware of all the options.

Consider appropriate treatments

Having arrived at some initial proposals about the style and scale of expenditure required by the production, it is then possible to make allowance for the appropriate treatments:

- How much detail is necessary relative to the proposed lighting conditions?
- Which sets will be seen in the widest variety of lighting conditions?
- Which will be seen through the widest variety of multi-camera lenses?

Such sets obviously need careful preparation and specification in order to cover all the different conditions and problems that are likely to arise. Some may be seen only in very low-key conditions, where surface texture is of the greatest importance to the scene. In other sets there may be requirements to achieve better sound absorbing qualities on or under the floor treatment; or alternatively a set may have to take some extra-ordinary physical pressure — e.g. an actor crashes against the wall or door which therefore has to be reinforced with wood or steel supports as necessary to provide the solidity.

Decide on the key elements

The consideration of treatments leads on to an overview by the designer of what are considered to be the key elements within the production and design requirements — which scenes, which shots, which sets, which locations, which effects are the most important in the successful telling of the story? What order of priority do they assume in the overall realisation of the production? Gradually a picture can be built up where those elements that keep recurring as essential emerge and give a clear impression of the hierarchical structure of important characters, scenes, set and locations.

Decide on the essential demands of the script

From this the designer can come to a judgement about what are the essential demands of the script and decide on the order of priorities concerning the importance of the various elements:

- As part of the story
- In creating the appropriate visual environment
- By the amount of inescapable construction
- By the quantity, quality, rarity, availability and manu-
  facture of props
- By commissioning experts to achieve various effects
- By assessing the resource and financial costs.

At this stage, the designer will be in the best position to discuss with the director the order of priorities being suggested and to explain the thinking behind them. This rank ordering is sometimes wholly accepted, but at other times it does happen that the director and designer have different views on the importance of certain scenes and the emphasis they are to be given within the concept and style. That is when the analysis above is of particular value, as it presents clearly the thinking and reasoning behind the design proposals.

This analysis enables a creative discussion to take place between the director and designer in which they can more easily decide on an agreed approach which will be followed throughout the entire production.

CONSIDER THE PRE-RECORDING/SHOOTING SCHEDULE

Bearing in mind this sense of priorities, it is now time for the designer to look at the production manager's proposed recording or shooting schedule, and see how it compares with the requirements that are emerging from the initial design proposals. In a studio recording these may involve change-rounds of sets from one day to the next, with floors to be re-painted or laid, re-sets of scenery or props during the recording (or rehearse/recording). When shooting on location, there are logistical problems of the whereabouts of props, the availability of craft and props effort and the time needed to prepare locations, as well as the necessity for contingency plans in case the schedule is badly disrupted by a totally unexpected event. The cardinal rule in television — that pre-planning is all important, even if (and especially when) that plan is known to be subject to further change and will certainly be departed from once the shoot starts — comes into its own in these circumstances.

Work out a running order

The initial recording order or the film shooting schedule (which at this early stage of the realisation process can only be based on the information available to the production manager at the time) is likely to be able to show little more than the broad parameters. These will include the number of studio recording days, whether or not the pattern is rehearse/record, whether or not provision has been made for set and prop changes or overnight turn-rounds; alternatively on film, the length of the overall shoot, whether stages or studios are being used and whether there are any locations that have already been fixed.

The designer then needs to inject into that equation the design factors and see what effect they have on the result. According to the priorities that are emerging and the work entailed, additional time may be required for preparatory work to be carried out or for travelling time to and from locations. The director and designer may have changed originally designated locations into studio interiors or *vice versa*, which can make an enormous difference to the arrangement of the schedule or recording order; re-builds and prop re-setting requires time, as does attention to continuity.

At this stage the designer needs to concentrate on incorporating the prioritised design requirements into the schedule unequivocally, and then consult with the production manager to feed back the implications of the changes that are being considered. It is simpler to carry out the exercise this way rather than try to anticipate the responses of a number of different people.

This leads on to a further process of adjustment, as the other members of the team are carrying out similar exercises with similar implications for the schedule or recording order, and there may well need to be further detailed negotiations about the set/location list according to what the director and designer want and what the total servicing implications are on the schedule.

Re-evaluate the studio/location and/or the interior/exterior shooting list

In the light of the developing design and shooting schedule, certain sets or locations will inevitably pose problems which in turn will necessitate the re-assessment of the initial studio/location breakdown list. The director and designer need to consider each set and location and decide with the location manager what is their preferred option at that stage. Considerations will have to be made on the assumptions that certain locations can be found within a certain radius and area, which in turn dictates the amount of travel to be undertaken by the unit and the amount of time needed to move and to set up ready to shoot. If it is not possible to find all the necessary locations in the right area and close enough to each other, then it may be more cost effective to build the missing one rather than go on looking; or alternatively, accept the need for additional travel and potential time loss by using a location that is further afield.

RECCE FOR LOCATIONS

Whether the programme being made is a comedy, which is usually recorded in a studio in front of an audience but has a few filmed or video inserts of location sequences, or whether it is a full-scale drama being made entirely on location, the next step is to make a 'recce' or reconnaissance — a pre-filming visit to the locations in order to assess them for script requirements, visual suitability, access, facilities, permissions to film, etc.

Roles of director and designer on the recce

The director and designer will be concerned with the dramatic feel rather than pin-point accuracy when deciding upon locations. For example, when working on a dramatised re-construction of historical events, the actual location may present physical difficulties (of scale, for instance, or more simply that its architecture and interior have been radically altered) which make it virtually impossible to shoot.

Again, it may be desirable to find acceptably similar architectural or geographical features in one part of the country, rather than transport the unit long distances to the actual spot; a classic example of this was in the BBC Wales production of *The New World* where the coast of New England was found outside Cardiff rather than across the Atlantic ocean.

Production manager and location manager roles

Depending on the size, complexity and run-up time available on the production, the director is likely to be too busily engaged with casting and planning to be able to spend much time looking for locations. This is where the production manager or more recently on dramas, the location manager takes on the task of finding and shortlisting suitable locations, based on a brief from the director and designer about the dramatic feel and the architectural style or historical period called for by the script.

Often designers will also become involved, as they have built up their own knowledge of locations used in the past, and sometimes their planning is seriously held up until key locations are agreed upon. The director is then presented with a selected list of the most likely option(s) to go and view, together with the production manager or location manager as the case may be and the designer. A decision is then taken bearing in mind all the needs of the script and the unit.

The designer's involvement on location is helped enormously by the location manager, because making the necessary visual alterations to a location or area involves two basic principles — one is visually to add to the location, and the other is to take away or disguise those things that are out of place. In carrying out this task it is essential to gain the necessary permissions from, for instance, the police, companies, local authorities, local residents or next-door neighbours of the property being used. This is an important part of the job of the location manager.

While the designer will be concerned with planning and working out the techniques of disguising those features that may be out of period, by building, or covering, or painting, taping or even removing and then replacing certain items, the location manager will be concerned with obtaining the permissions.

Another vital part of the job is arranging for the removal of visual anomalies such as television aerials, estate agents' boards, and even cars and lorries that are out of period, so that the designer's additive work is not compromised by incongruous eyesores and the maximum production value can be obtained by being able to shoot the newly dressed location as comprehensively as possible.

Practicalities to be considered at potential locations
On those occasions when the designer has to recce without the location manager or production manager, the practicalities of a location have to be borne in mind as well as its appearance. Account must be taken of access for all vehicles, not simply the designer's car and the craft van; there might be generator vehicles, props van, a hydraulic lift vehicle for a camera mounting, catering van and trailer as well as a 50-seater passenger coach for artists and extras. And, having got all these vehicles to the site, they (together with all the unit cars) have to be parked. There might also be the need to maintain through traffic. Also it is not uncommon for services such as electricity and water to be required on the site.

Notes and records
When recce-ing it is always sensible for a designer to take photographs, whether polaroid or standard film, or even to use a small video camera. Such a record can be of crucial importance in demonstrating to the director the type of shots — both establishing and developing — the designer has envisaged. Also, a video of the location can be processed with a digital video paint system in order to test out the possibility of effects shots and demonstrate to the director how the overall frame will compose. Diagrams of the site plan are made with the positions of camera shots indicated with special notes being

*Page 86: Visual effects being prepared on location in Thetford Forest for the battle of Waterloo scene in **Vanity Fair***

made of 'impossible' masking problems presented at each site, and the line up of camera shots necessary to avoid them.

Site survey and recce

An accurate site survey by the designer will probably not be made until the location is decided upon and has been success-fully negotiated by the location manager. At that stage, the key camera shots will have been decided, and those areas that need to be accurately measured and surveyed will be known to the designer. That is when more detailed notes will be made and more detailed photographs taken as necessary to make easier the problem of visual continuity — the matching details from one location to another, or matching a location shot to a studio or stage set built and shot some time later.

An accurate site plan of the location(s) (the equivalent to the studio plan) will be drawn up to a suitable scale and, where necessary, each different set-up drawn individually indicating the details of scenery, properties and effects required in particular scenes or shots.

INITIAL ASSESSMENT OF COSTS

While all the above stages of designing, planning and preparation have been taking place, the designer will have had a good intuitive idea of the running costs and the resource implications of each particular set or location, based mainly upon previous experience or, where necessary, by obtaining advice from the construction manager, buyers or specialist contractors and suppliers. Knowing beforehand the number of locations involved, the designer will also have an idea of whether or not the proposed budget bears a close relationship to the proposed location list and shooting schedule.

This is the time when the first idea of reasonably accurate cost can be obtained. It has to be assumed that a firm list of sets/locations has been decided upon by the director and designer, and that the production manager's schedule is starting to take a much more definite shape, based upon a

This location sketch plan for *The Secret Agent* shows a tracing paper overlay of the set taped on to a drawing of the BBC Elstree car park that was used as a lot.

substantial amount of information from all members of the production team, and upon the locations that have been negotiated and agreed upon by the location manager. Also, the designer's ideas and proposals are by now becoming more definite and as this happens it becomes easier to quantify and cost the realisation of the design concept.

A cost is put against each set or location, broken down into its elements of construction, specialist effort, and properties costs; then the sets can be grouped together as dictated by the locations or composite sets in the studio. The breakdown of construction costs will include hours to be worked (including overtime hours) and materials to be used, on a daily basis.

Finally, any other items not included in the set list are added, together with a contingency sum and, when appropriate, design fees and expenses are included in the overall costs.

This breakdown of costs allows effective monitoring to take place later and indicates immediately how the incurred costs are comparing with the original estimates or quotations. It also means that if the overall cost exceeds the given budget the designer knows where the main areas of cost are being incurred and can decide relatively easily where any cuts have to be made.

The other element of design costing to be taken into account is that of running expenses as opposed to the costs of sets and props; designs sometimes require the continuing use of resources, craft or stage effort, special transport or other support facilities. If the production is being made under the umbrella of a large organisation or company, these costs may or may not be directly included in the designer's costs, and sometimes even end up as corporate costs or costs paid for by the production rather than the designer; if on the other hand the programme is being made by an independent production company then the chances are that the running costs will be directly attributed to the design budget and the designer made responsible for them. Either way they are not to be forgotten.

DESIGN RESPONSE

Until now the designer has been researching, reading, talking, thinking, evaluating, costing, and planning in something of a cyclical pattern, absorbing each piece of new information and adjusting the whole proposal as necessary to include the new element. By this stage, the time has come to gather together all the strands into one response to the production requirements. As we have seen already, these strands include the following areas:

- Script/programme idea/subject treatment
- Research material gathered and selected
- Script breakdown carried out
- Director's requirements elicited
- Design ideas prepared
- Key shots decided
- Technical facilities noted
- Proposed recording/shooting schedule noted
- Safety requirements incorporated
- Given budget noted.

When the director poses a question or puts forward an alternative possibility to be considered, almost every angle will have been anticipated and the designer can provide a well-considered and informed answer or alternative proposal as the case may be.

Communication with the director

The next question to arise is how to communicate this information? The first thing to say is not to swamp the director with too much detail at once, but to provide information on a 'needs-to-know' basis. In the same way that the designer has worked through a complex process before formulating proposals, so the information needs to be presented coherently, explaining along the way the reasons for key decisions and for the proposed visual style, the adoption of which is one of the most important decisions facing any production team.

Assuming that the director has agreed the design concept and approach, there is every reason for the designer to proceed with the realisation and implementation of the design without referring back to the director more than is absolutely necessary.

Obviously this question of how to convey a design in the best possible manner is a very personal matter and will vary with each designer.

Visual research material
Have the key selected items ready and available for the director to see, for example, in relation to a part of the script or to the visual style as a whole. It is sometimes better to invite the director to visit the design, especially if there is a considerable amount of visual material already displayed and available to view. The other advantage is that the director is a little further away from the 'phone than is the case in the production office and interruptions are a little less likely.

Notes in the script:
Before going to the meeting, the designer should know those places in the script where notes have been made that either need to be given to the director or are questions that require answers.

First impressions:
In discussing the style of the production, first impressions gained when reading the script are of the utmost importance and are very valuable to the dialogue between the director and designer in their search for the visual style.

As already mentioned under the script breakdown, these need to be noted and/ or remembered.

Conceptual sketches and models:
First impressions of the visualisation of a set, location or scene will frequently be translated into sketches and models and, at this stage, they can be embryonic and also in a form that can still be malleable and subject to radical change if necessary.

Card models still provide a quick and easy method of conveying the concept of a set to the director. They can easily be altered and cut around when necessary at the early planning stage

Storyboard jottings:
Another method of conveying initial impressions is to indicate the key shots and sequences and how they will develop by using storyboard jottings. This can be done quickly when reading through the script and referred to later for more detailed analysis and refinement. Storyboard jottings can also be useful, not only in the more important shots and scenes, but also whenever the designer feels for various reasons that there is the need to explain the sequence of shooting within a set or location in order to make a serious storytelling point.

Key shots:
Key shots are those which contain vital information for the viewer — either to do with the visual style or with telling the story — or both; they have a dramatic significance or may be known in advance to be difficult to shoot and therefore deserve special attention in their planning and realisation.

Key sequences can often include the master shot that establishes the geography of a set or location, together with camera positions and shots providing close-ups or cutaways later; both aspects need to be covered equally satisfactorily.

Key shots and sequences can be likened to milestones and signposts that are set up to enable journeys to take place, but not necessarily by the same route.

Perspectives:
Perspectives, or 'visuals' as they are called, provide the director with invaluable information concerning the set and the characters. Some designers produce beautiful rendered drawings that are not only works of art in themselves but enable the details of style and dressing to be worked out as the drawing progresses. They can provide wonderfully atmospheric impressions of what a scene should feel like and what it is likely to look like. Other designers rely on simpler, quicker sketches with which to convey the essence of their design. CAD is enormously useful in this respect as it can present accurate per- spectives to convey factually what will and will not be seen and thus save much debate about what is and what is not possible.

Rough plans:
Rough plans are the initial plans which the designer draws to scale having gathered together as much background information as possible. Usually they are drawn individually for each set on separate pieces of tracing paper and then composed into a rough studio plan which shows the designer's preferred configuration of sets planned to fit into the studio or location facility (see p.89).

At this stage it is still relatively easy for the director and designer to change individual plans as well as the overall studio layout to take account of differences in scale, size and interpretation. At the same time the 'rough' plans have to be sufficiently accurate to be able to judge what shots are possible and whether physical dimensions (of say, furniture or other large items) can be properly accommodated.

Costings:
At this stage, the designer needs to have a sufficiently good idea of outline costings to be able to discuss with the director the financial viability of the design proposals being presented as well as alternative approaches or treatments and their respective cost implications. This knowledge is gained largely from experience and from other support members of the team, but if necessary, for instance with some essential and unusual facility or artefact, initial estimates can be obtained direct from the specialist contractor or supplier. More detailed costings come later in the design process.

Obtain director's approval
Out of this comprehensive presentation of ideas and debate with the director, the designer needs to obtain agreement to the design proposals. Sometimes approval is given to the complete design, and at other times it is confirmed only after some discussion which results in making a number of amendments or alterations until the two can arrive at a mutually acceptable design solution.

This is then used to up-date the rough plan into the agreed plan and to up-date and alter as necessary any conceptual models (finished models usually materialise after the drawings have been completed).

Consult with other experts
When the designer is planning the studio or location, allowance has to be made for all the other technical teams, so that they can make their individual contributions with sufficient space to do so, especially for lighting, sound and cameras.

Equally important is the need for the designer to consult readily with the other professionals on the unit in order to produce the best possible solutions for the programme. Creative teamwork is the most effective way of realising television programmes, working closely together to achieve results, rather than by fortuitous accident. The main categories involved are likely to include:

- Lighting (film cameraman or lighting director)
- Sound (film recordist or sound supervisor)
- Musical director
- Choreographer
- Graphic design
- Costume design
- Make-up
- Visual effects
- Video effects
- CAD/design effects
- Safety

These consultations are presumed to be confirmation of pre-liminary conversations that will have taken place earlier in the production preparation period. Sometimes this consultative process is possible in a planning meeting — usually the case in large companies and broadcasting organisations whose operations depend on pre-planning in order to make a number of productions simultaneously. If a large-scale planning meeting is not possible, then the consultations will have to take place as best they may, but take place they must if the right amount of co-operation and smooth working is to be achieved during the shoot.

FINALISE DESIGN REQUIREMENTS
Having agreed the design concept and plan with the director and the other members of the team, the designer is then able to draw up a clear brief to work from; the time is right to finalise

the design requirements and change them from a clearly stated concept into scale drawings and specifications that can be draughted, specified, costed and made.

Preparing drawings and specifications

Drawing styles will differ according to the company organisation and traditions and the workshop(s) that will be making the scenery. The universal scale that is used in television is 1:50; it has a familiarity that comes with long practice and all members of the production team are by now used to reading studio plans and elevations at that scale. After a short time, most television designers can draw to that scale without the aid of a scale rule!

Construction drawings are sometimes drawn, as in architecture, using sections and elevations, but most often the convention of an extended elevation is adopted, in which the walls of a set are extended outwards in a continuous line; this is usually explained as having two purposes. Firstly, that by sticking the paper on to card, cutting out and bending the elevations, a simple but extremely effective scale model can be made quickly and easily and, secondly, that it is easier for designers and contractors to estimate costs of scenery worked out on a foot-run basis.

Plans and elevations

Drawings are prepared in the form of plans and elevations, and studio or location plans. Each set or location is first drawn in plan form, (working from the agreed scale plans presented to the director as a rough studio or location plan and agreed or amended), and then the elevations are drawn up from the information on the plan, together with heights and other details.

When these construction drawings are finished, the plans from these are traced at a later stage (unless a CAD system is being used when creating a copy takes little more than a few minutes) on to studio plans in their final agreed positions. The term 'plan' or 'floor plan' generally refers to the complete studio plan containing all the sets rather than the individual plan of a set.

*Pages 99-101: The scale plan and elevation of Verloc's shop for **The Secret Agent** set are annotated and supplemented with larger scale or full size drawings in order to explain construction details; see details A, B, C, D*

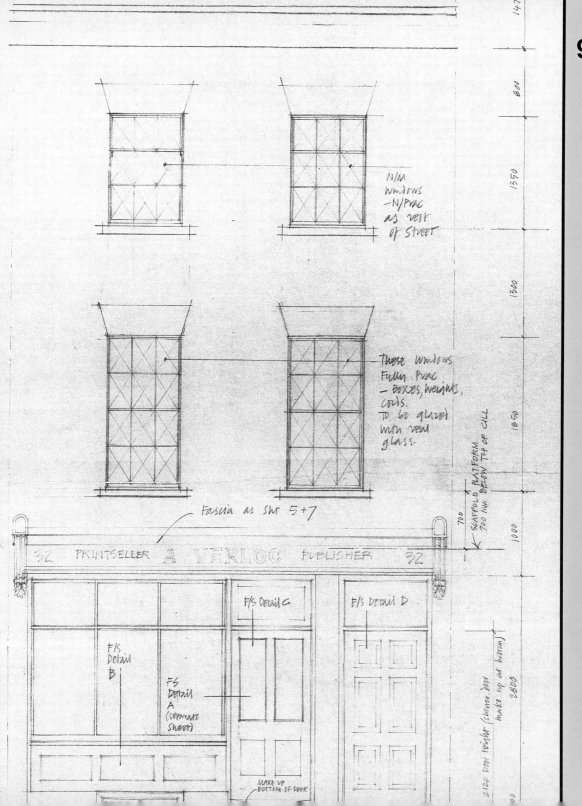

N/M Windows
— N/Prac
as rest
of street

These windows
Fully Prac
— boxes, weights,
cords.
To be glazed
with real
glass.

Fascia as Sht 5+7

700

SCAFFOLD PLATFORM
700 MM BELOW TOP OF CILL

32   PRINTSELLER   A VERLOG   PUBLISHER   32

F/S Detail C

F/S Detail D

F/S
Detail
B

F/S
Detail
A
(separate
sheet)

MAKE UP
BOTTOM OF DOOR

2120 Door Height (Shorter door
make up at bottom)

1475

800

1350

1300

1050

1000

2800

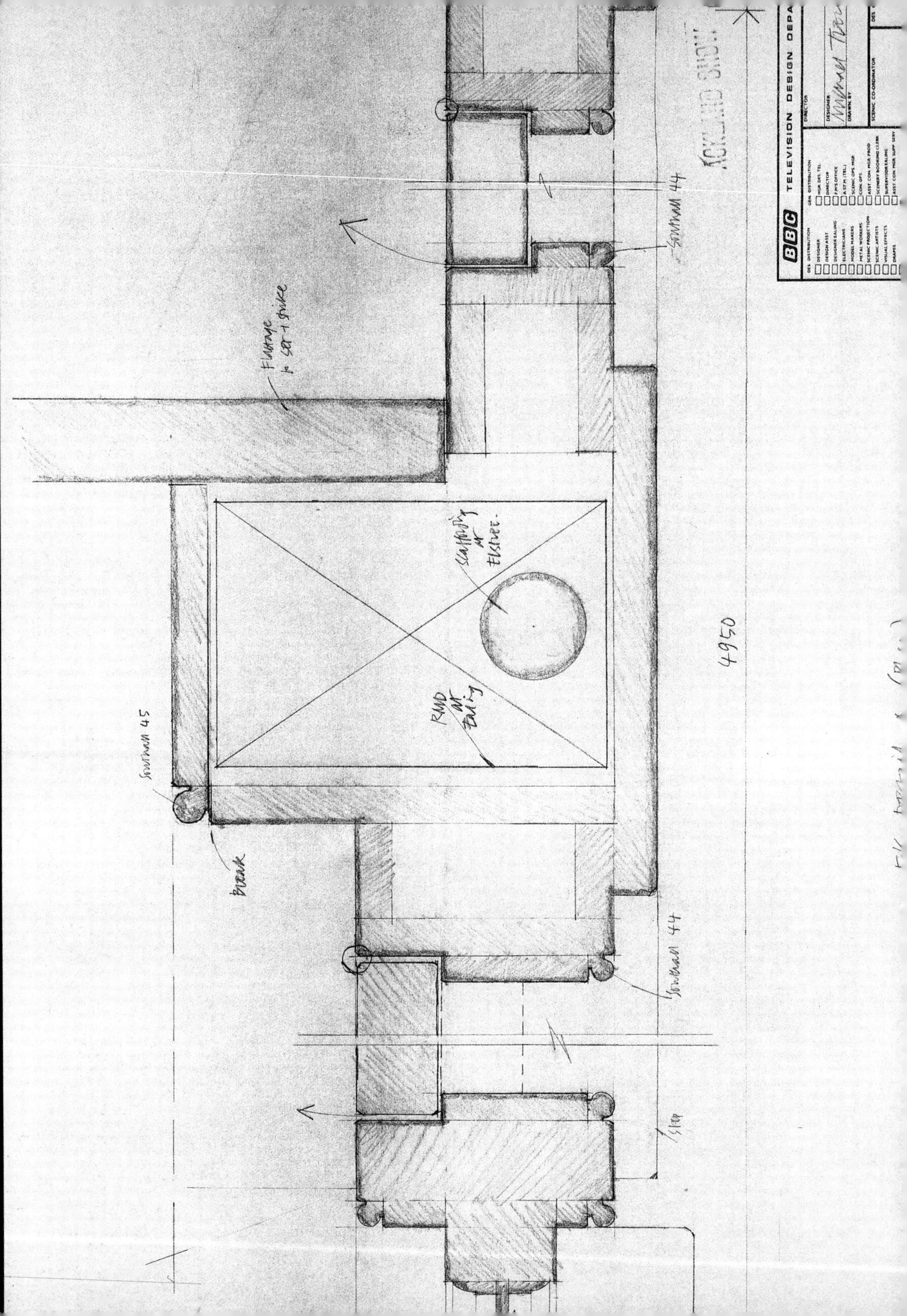

BBC TELEVISION DESIGN DEPA

DIRECTOR
DESIGNER   William Ter
DRAWN BY
SCENIC COORDINATOR

ACKLAND SHOW.

Sonanna 44

Flange to set + spike

Scaffolding on Fisher.

Rmd w batg.

4950

Sonanna 45

break

Sonanna 44

step

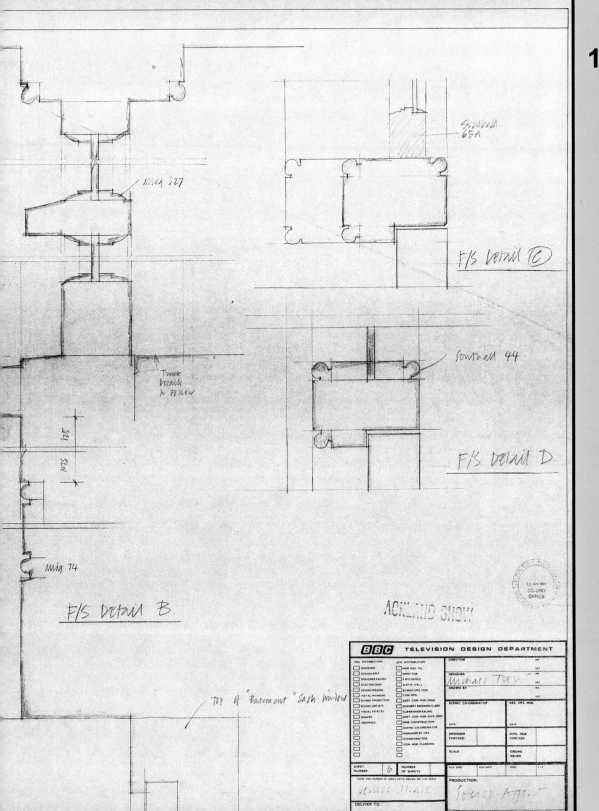

Mldg 327

Track
details
to follow

125

NTS

Mldg 74

F/S Detail B.

Southall 65A

F/S Detail C

Southall 44.

F/S Detail D

TOP of "Basement" Sash window

ACKLAND SNOW

13 NOV 1991
CO-ORD
OFFICE

BBC	TELEVISION DESIGN DEPARTMENT		
DES. DISTRIBUTION	GEN. DISTRIBUTION	DIRECTOR	
☐ DESIGNER	☐ MGR. DES. TEL.		
☐ DESIGN ASST	☐ DIRECTOR	DESIGNER	
☐ DESIGNER EALING	☐ F/M's OFFICE	Michael Trevor	
☐ ELECTRICIANS	☐ A.ST. M. (TEL)	DRAWN BY	
☐ MODELMAKERS	☐ SCENIC OPS. MGR.		
☐ METAL WORKERS	☐ CON. OPS.		
☐ SCENIC PROJECTION	☐ ASST CON. MGR. PROD	SCENIC CO-ORDINATOR	DES. OPS MGR.
☐ SCENIC ARTISTS	☐ SCENERY BOOKING CLERK		
☐ VISUAL EFFECTS	☐ SUPERVISOR EALING		
☐ DRAPES	☐ ASST. CON. MGR. SUPP. SERV	DATE	DATE
☐ GRAPHICS	☐ MGR. CONSTRUCTION		
☐	☐ SCENIC CO-ORDINATOR	DESIGNER	DWG. MGR.
☐	☐ MANAGER ST. OPS	CHECKED	CHECKED
☐	☐ O/CONTRACTOR		
☐	☐ CON. MGR. PLANNING	SCALE	GREENS ISSUED
SHEET NUMBER 6	NUMBER OF SHEETS	FILM ZERO	FILM DATE	ZERO	
NAME AND NUMBER OF SERIES SET(S) DRAWN ON THIS SHEET		PRODUCTION:	
Venice House		Soviet Agent	
DELIVER TO:			

Floor finishes and supplementary details

Floor finishes can involve elaborate designs and colours, with considerable details to be conveyed. When that is the case it is worth preparing a separate drawing for this purpose and sometimes a separate floor plan to avoid an over-complicated studio plan which in the end will not be the best means of conveying the appropriate amount of detail and setting out information.

In the drawing and building of scenery, it is often the case that a greater degree of detail is needed than is possible at the 1:50 scale of the elevations, and within the space available on the page. In that case, supplementary details are drawn up at bigger scales as appropriate — 1:20 or 1:10 or even full size if necessary, to explain a particular piece of structure or intricate finish.

CAD

If the designer or the organisation (or both) has a computer-aided design system, then depending upon the extent, nature and purpose of that system and of the programme being made, it will almost certainly come into play at this stage. CAD is discussed at greater length later in the book, but in producing drawings for television its main value can be seen in its facility for making copies and alterations, producing drawings by making copies of stock items in a 'library', so that, for example, the regular and repetitive production of floor plans that are not quite the same, but which need re-issuing is very easily and quickly achieved with the minimum of effort. On the other hand, there are many drawings of a 'one-off' nature that would still be more easily and quickly drawn by hand, rather than by individual designers spending additional time learning how to use a computer draughting software package, or having to use computer operators.

Computer 'libraries' can save much time by removing the need to re-draw scenic items each time they are used and instead simply copy and assemble them quickly and easily into a new drawing; but if the scenic item is a newly-created shape it is much more debatable as to whether there is any significant saving or not, especially when the frequency of use of the computer system by the designer and therefore familiarity and speed of operation is taken into account.

Television designers are often obliged to use stock elements, but all the time are striving to use them in an individual fashion; computers are at their best when working on repetitive tasks. Effectiveness of one method or another all depends on the nature of the programme and the design concept being pursued.

Finished model to be made

Once the construction drawings are finished, by hand or computer, the finished model can be built, as explained earlier, by using the drawn elevations cut out and stuck down on to their plan.This is an important event, as it shows exactly how the designs will look, in a manner that is understood by everyone, regardless of their familiarity with draughting conventions and scale drawings.

If the drawings have been carried out on a computer, it would be possible, given the appropriate drawing and/or modelling programme, to generate perspective views ranging from either simple 'wire frame' perspective drawings up to fully rendered and lit views, corresponding to camera positions and shots. It may be that in some cases this form of presentation, and particularly that linked to video images will outstrip the humble cardboard model that has served directors and designers for so many years.

Draw up props list

Armed with a new set of construction drawings and the model (or computer perspectives), the designer can settle down to look in complete detail at the props that will be needed, and list them so that none of the key props are forgotten. Procedures surrounding the actual listing of props will vary with different organisations and very much from television to film, but props buyers will often be delegated by the designer to select props according to a brief and, in the end, it is the designer's responsibility to ensure that all the props look right and fit into the agreed design concept. To this end it is essential that the designer knows fully what is required. A simple way to ensure that this happens is to list, set by set and then break down, within each set, into sections headed, for example, furniture, small props, and any other convenient categories that will assist the initial coverage and subsequent acquisition of all the props that are required.

Chapter 5

Budget and Costs

When starting on a new project, the designer may be asked either to design within a given budget or to assist in assessing what the budget should be and what it is possible to achieve in design terms. These are two sides of the same coin and, although different in approach, are the same in principle; either way, the producer and director need to know that their plans can be realised within a given budget or, alternatively, that their proposals as initially costed by the designer provide a figure that is within acceptable financial limits to the production as a whole.

The designer will be expected to have a good idea of costings as the project develops; this assessment comes from previous experience of similar productions and from expert advice where necessary.

When costing a design, it is sensible first to break down the costs into the basic elements of scenic construction and set-ting, props and transport, and then to identify any other items that require specific attention — for example, a large-scale location shoot supposedly taking place in another country may call for a large amount of graphic street signage and posters and as such may command a separate budget item.

Further sub-division can then take place into specialist sup-pliers or facilities in construction or properties, and then into smaller units, e.g. clearly identified individual sets or locations or groups of sets or locations. These easily identifiable unit costs then provide an essential basis from which to make budget adjustments when required in the planning stages.

What does the design budget cover?

From the *producer's* point of view the idea of a fixed price design budget is an ideal solution, as it implies that the design concept will be realised without an overspend or a series of requests for additional resources. From the *designer's* point of view the idea of working to a fixed price design budget would be a realistic proposition only if it were linked directly to a fixed set of production requirements which have been agreed, will remain constant and can therefore be priced and brought to realisation.

In reality these two sets of ideals exist only rarely and even when they do last minute changes are usually made during the production rehearsal period and throughout the shoot. These adjustments are of the essence of high-quality programme making and, as long as they are anticipated and kept within budgetary limits, are essential ingredients. However, without some degree of scope the production team would soon become forced into making decisions based on the prohibitive cost of resources, rather than an assessment of the intrinsic importance and value to the original production idea of realising such changes. In many smaller productions, unfortunately, this process is the norm.

This is not to argue that there should be limitless flexibility and additional cost, but simply to underline the need for contingency planning in order to provide flexibility and recognition from the production team that unexpected problems have to be dealt with as affecting the whole production and not simply design.

Visual cost effectiveness
A good designer should be well aware of visual cost effectiveness instinctively. This does not mean providing the cheapest solution available at every opportunity, but rather making sure that the maximum production value is obtained from the scenic, props and specialist items provided within the design realisation. To ensure that this happens requires careful pre-planning, sometimes a great deal of persuasion and, on other occasions, may even require an acceptance by the designer that apparent waste is considered by the production team to be an acceptable price to pay. Occasionally, for instance, in the case of topical current affairs or magazine programmes, a designer's work may not even be seen at all, despite having been specially constructed and brought to the studio, because of an editorial decision to omit the item concerned. This is the exception rather than the rule, but may be considered necessary if editorial choice of content matter is to be maintained.

Planning to be seen

Another pursuit of the designer in achieving visual cost effec-tiveness is to 'plan to see' — not only the key shots, but also the elements and items or props within those shots. A key prop that is important to the story, to a character or to the atmos-phere of a scene obviously must be seen if it is to play its part and to have its desired effect on the audience. How often have there been wonderful prop items in the studio, even in the sets themselves, that in the event did not register on the screen because they did not quite get into shot at the appropriate moment, or alternatively lurked half in and half out of a pool of shadow and were lost. Planning to be seen can avoid this problem.

As is always the case in television production, the achievement of any objective entails pre-planning and sometimes negotia-tion with the respective members of the production team to ensure that the circumstances are right to capture the essence of a particular scenic item, effect or prop within the context of a key shot or scene. Of course, the successful achievement of this objective not only avoids wasting money, but also avoids the alternative to pre-planning that means surrendering control and leaving everything to chance.

Changes

Changes to production requirements are inevitable in television and the designer must be ready to respond creatively and constructively when the moment comes, as come it most certainly will. The designer's response to requests for changes will depend upon the initial budgeting and the nature of the provision for contingencies and indeed whether cuts have to be made in order to finance the latest change or a new requirement.

Generally speaking, alterations and extras can be provided by the designer right up to the last moment before shooting. However, they all cost money — usually the later the change or addition is made the more money — and it is often only after the heat of the moment that the 'programme imperative' may seem to be less important than it did when the change was demanded. This is an area where there needs to be a clear understanding from the outset between the designer and the production team, in order to avoid talk of overspends and perhaps even enforced production cuts.

Relative visual production values
During the whole process of realising a design for television, the designer will be constantly re-evaluating the visual import-ance of the different elements that go to make up a design. The contributory factors that go towards assessing this are many and varied; they range from the straightforward dramatic and visual significance, to the related factor of cost and the more complex issue of the knock-on effect that achieving a particular item could have on the shooting schedule and overall produc-tion requirements. The resulting list of priorities will need to be re-assessed in the light of prevailing circumstances, so that the visual production value of a scene, element or prop has to be seen as relative to the successful realisation of the overall production.

Therefore, the designer should have a clear idea of the relative visual production values of all the key scenes, scenic items and props in order to be able to respond quickly to a proposed re-scheduling of the shooting or any other budgetary problem that calls for a radical re-evaluation.

Preparation time
Materials used in the construction of sets are expensive, as are small props and furniture used to dress those sets, and both elements deserve to be used in such a way that their visual effectiveness and cost are fully exploited. Not only is it perfectly possible to pre-plan television productions, but it is true to say that over the past twenty-five years this has been accepted as the most effective way of doing things. However, in more recent times the preparation period required for pre-planning is not always seen as an economic necessity and sometimes is even rejected as being an unnecessarily high expense. This is a very short-sighted view, as pre-planning is the best way of ensuring

that the maximum visual and dramatic effect can be gained when using the lowest possible level of money and resources.

Appropriate use of materials and props

By pre-planning camera shots and their composition with the director, the designer can predict much more accurately the appropriate use of detailing, materials and props, and as a result savings are possible and much unnecessary expenditure can be avoided. If, for instance, a constant very low key lighting level can be agreed for certain sets, then dressing props and materials do not need to be of such high quality and cost as when the scene is high key and brightly lit. However, if unavoidable hitches have occurred in the shooting so that pre-planning is cut down to the minimum — usually a quick meeting the night before — then there is no opportunity to choose the quality of detailing, materials and dressings and the designer simply provides as much 'cover' for the camera as the money allows. Whether or not all this effort is seen on the screen, hardly seen due to dramatic lighting, or not seen at all due to a completely new camera position decided on the day, is unavoidably left to chance.

Avoid the unachievable

Another key piece of advice for designers in the planning stage of a production is to reject ideas that are clearly unachievable, for whatever reason, be they stylistic, safety, financial, logistic or whatever. It is far more sensible to spend time offering and discussing alternatives rather than trying to make an idea work that is clearly impossible. Directors would prefer to get a clear response, even if negative, than live with a gradually diminishing possibility and later inherit a less convenient but inevitable change.

Always come back to the original idea

In all these deliberations, the designer — and the whole production team for that matter — need to keep firmly in mind the programme idea while referring back to the script requirements so that they do not become too strongly influenced by cost implications linked to ease of achievement. This direction leads to comfortable mediocrity, rather than creative tension and the achievement of the highest possible quality.

Responsibility for the budget

It is true to say that some designers never seem to have budgetary problems at all and sail through their programmes unfettered, whereas others have to work much harder at designing within their budget. Regardless of which camp they come from, all designers must carry full responsibility for their budget, as they alone can make the initial assessments, necessary adjustments and re-arrangements to achieve an acceptable design concept within the limits of time, resources and cash.

If the designer is a freelance working for an independent production company, there is perhaps less likelihood of a budgetary problem arising than in a larger television company or organisation. This is due to the fact that there is much less chance of any misunderstanding in the smaller context, because the self-interests of most people on the production team cause them to anticipate problems of overspending. In any case, future work is most likely to depend on known reputation.

However, in larger organisations and companies, budgetary dealings may be much foggier. Budgetary matters are often only nominally assigned to the designer, without the accompanying authority and choice to go with them. In reality the responsibility for a particular resource or facility can remain with other managers who have different interests (usually corporate) at heart which can soon conflict with the demands of individual programmes. It is possible for several individuals on the production team to have notional interests in the same production budget, but for no one person to have complete responsibility.

Construction manager

Usually, the construction manager will be the first contact the designer makes in starting to assemble costs for a production. Construction and assembly costs frequently account for the major part of the design budget and, for that very reason, it is important to establish early in the design process what proportion of the available resources to allow. Within the construction area the costs readily break down into headings that recur on the vast majority of productions, and they provide a natural and useful subdivision of costs and the opportunity to consider priorities when assessing the overall budget.

Pre-fabricated (workshop) scenic work

Typically, this might involve sets being built for a studio recording, which is a clearly-defined parcel of work. The final price will depend on the amount of time involved, how late are the drawings (a regular hazard), the choice of materials and whether or not the required zero date necessitates overtime being worked. Items which may or may not be included will vary considerably according to the organisation or company that is producing the programme.

Large organisations might have their own transport and various craft skills on their permanent staff, and also might have stock resources such as props and scenery that are available for use. Independent production companies would simply pay for everything they need as they go, hiring or purchasing as appropriate, as none of the resources would be available on a stand-by basis.

The important thing for the designer to be sure of is that all aspects of the construction costs have been covered regardless, which system is being used. The final cost of scenic construction can, of course, vary enormously depending on the amount of 'free' resources being provided, and it is important to remember to establish a well-defined baseline before comparing costs.

On-site (location) scenic work

Alternatively, pre-fabricated (workshop) scenic work could involve scenery being pre-fabricated in order to be assembled on site. In this case it would probably be costed out as part of the location servicing construction budget, as it would probably involve a major build on location and would be treated and costed as such.

When planning this type of work, the onus is on the construction manager and designer to work out a schedule that covers all the construction requirements. They work from the designer's breakdown of the agreed locations, assessing the amount of craft effort needed for each setting and then translating that into work schedules (including basic time and overtime) planned for the carpenters, painters, plasterers, scenic artists and other skills involved. Pre-fabricated craft work may well be subcontracted if full scale workshop facilities are required, with the final assembly and finishing being carried out on site at the location.

Materials

The designer must consider very carefully the choice of materials to be used in the construction of scenery for television. Working in electronic studios usually requires that materials are suitably fire-proofed to a given specification determined by the local authority and fire brigade. This can sometimes impose limitations on the choice of the materials most commonly used — for example, timber, timber laminated boards, fibre boards, ply, laminated plastic, vacuum formed plastics, fibreglass, cyclorama materials, fabrics for drapes and furnishings, and so on. It is extremely important that such safety considerations are not ignored.

Also relevant is the saving on labour effected by using materials which would cut the time taken to employ traditional methods of construction. For example, it might be cheaper to make a panel of framed hardboard or ply, rather than use a ready surfaced fibre board. This could both speed up the manufacturing process as well as provide a higher quality finish.

Specialist contractors

In the provision of scenic construction, there are certain standard crafts that are usually readily available, either inside television companies or freelance; these will be scenic carpenters and painters, scenic artists, scenic sculptors, scenic plasterers, drapes and metalworkers.

Other services such as steelwork or scaffolding, glass-fibre moulding, plastic manufacture and vacuum forming, engineering metalwork manufacture and specialist rigging imply the need for engaging experts in those fields, because television requires their services only occasionally. When using specialist contractors, one of the most important aspects to consider from the earliest stages is how their contribution is to fit into the overall timetable.

The other key consideration is whether they are considered to be sub-contractors of the main contractor, or whether they are separate contractors, in which case the construction manager or designer is responsible for co-ordinating the overall work plan. This can mean considerable work in monitoring both progress and budget lines to ensure the right quality is being delivered within cost and on time.

Production buyer
Along with the construction manager, the other person the designer will contact in the early stages of a production will be the properties or production buyer. Along with construction, properties costs frequently form a major part of a production. On certain occasions they can be greater than the construction costs if there is limited building but extensive dressing on location. Whereas construction costs generally account for the greater share of the design budget, at least it is possible to plan in advance and identify the likely costs fairly accurately, whereas the properties budget is much more volatile and liable to last-minute fluctuations.

There are many reasons for this, but the main problem lies in the availability or otherwise of props — when they are wanted and their price. At the stage of writing out the props list, the designer might well know the props that would meet the requirement in terms of style, cost and availability, and could even order them to be reserved by one of the suppliers, but when the time comes some of the items may be damaged or lost as a result of a previous booking — for example, a set of chairs — and this in turn means that an alternative selection must be made, based on a choice from chairs available at the time.

When this happens, the designer obviously has to re-assess the prop priorities with the production buyer and be ready to take some difficult decisions in order to achieve the necessary re-adjustment of the original budget figure. Bearing in mind that this situation can easily occur several times on the same production and in the case of key props, on a scale that goes beyond the design area alone, props costs can suddenly and all too easily become a production problem as well as a design problem.

Breakdown of prop priorities
When the designer first meets the production buyer, one of the most important things to establish is a clear brief for the buyer to follow when acquiring the props list, as it may well be the case that the designer does not accompany the buyer when hiring props. There are many variations on the process of acquiring props; at one end of the scale the AFM will be responsible not only for the acquisition but also for the transport and return, whereas at the other end there may be a production buyer and a set dresser working together with a prop master to manage the props on location, with transport being considered as a separate element altogether.

Regardless of the scale of operation, it is advisable for the designer to establish clearly a set of priorities when considering the provision of properties, so that when inevitable problems crop up during the buying process the answer can be decided upon as quickly as possible. It is sensible to structure the props list in such a manner that it pin-points the key areas of importance. A consistent style throughout the list makes life much easier when checking it at the suppliers to see that everything has been covered. One way of doing this is to group props into different categories in a hierarchical system, so that it is clear where and when they are to be used:

- On location or in a studio or stage
- Show dates and times as necessary
- Which set they belong to, and whether it is a new set or continuity — that is a set which already exists, the props for which are being held in store for impending use
- Differentiate between dressing and action props:

    Dressing props are those required to dress the set and are carefully chosen to convey to the audience particular aspects of the visual environment.

    Action props must also meet this requirement but particularly need the designer's approval because they are often seen in big close up — e.g. cups and drinking glasses, cutlery and hand-held props in general. They are called action props because they are concerned primarily with actors who will be using them as personal or hand props. As such they may need to be acquired in duplicate or triplicate in order to allow for quick re-takes, breakages, or even loss.

    Action props are the responsibility of the AFM to ensure they are available for the actors at the right time and right place on the set.

- Group the props under the headings of furniture, small props, soft goods, specialist suppliers, and use any other categories that are helpful in providing a comprehensive checklist for the designer and buyer to work from when acquiring props just prior to shooting.

Use of stock/hired/ borrowed/supplied/ props
The designer and buyer will usually have a very good knowledge of what props are available from the large range of suppliers around the London area and in other parts of the country. When working abroad, the situation is generally less favourable and the buyer and production team will need to research the area and availability of props before the shoot starts preparation. Even so, it can still be the case that the only

Fully practical fires require careful planning and control, as well as being made to conform to the fire and safety regulations.

The Dalek, which could be described either as a character or a fully practical prop, was made to the production designer's specifications by a prop maker

ACTION PROPS

Action props take many forms and often have to be specially made. Collapsible scenery and breakable props must be safe and should be made by special effects experts.

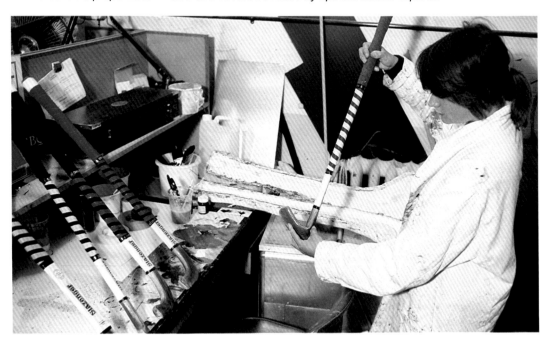

way to supply certain props may be to send them from Britain, rather then spend hours trying to find them locally. In some countries there is not the same tradition of companies hiring out to films, theatre and television.

Placement agencies

Although at present product placement is strictly illegal under BBC guidelines and the ITC code of sponsorship rules, there are nevertheless a number of companies supplying free products as props to the television industry and doing so perfectly legally. Fortunately, at the moment, and despite the ever-tightening programme budgets, the use of brands on British television remains discreet and there is a consensus view among buyers that they would rather buy props that are right for the scene rather than accept the wrong items simply because they are free. Even the branded prop agencies agree that if manufacturers were to start dictating the terms as they do in films, then productions would suffer, but more importantly they believe the audience is too sophisticated to accept the end result and would be likely to switch off — which would be good for nobody.

Transport on location

Transport, particularly on a large-scale location, is always a major component of the production budget and shooting schedule. There is no one way of organising it, as the most appropriate solution will depend very much on the individual circumstances surrounding the shoot. It may be sensible to engage transport for use by the whole production, or alternatively, it may be better to have dedicated transport for the construction team, and a separate prop van — especially if it is to be used as a mobile store while away from base. The main thing is for the designer to recognise the importance of transport arrangements and the cost and to make provision accordingly with the production manager.

CAD/design effects/post production areas

As soon as the designer recognises the need for CAD, design effects or post production work, the cost implications will need to be worked out and bid for with the director and producer. It is possible that some form of CAD may exist as part of an individual designer's personal equipment or, alternatively, that the company has a CAD system that can be made available to programme makers. Either way there are likely to be associated costs involved and perhaps it may be necessary to involve the use of a bureau in order to achieve certain output from the computer.

Producer
The producer generally gives the designer a budget and is the person who is ultimately responsible for the entire production. As the production moves through its various stages of preparation the producer will be involved at any stage where there is likely to be any significant shift in the use of cash or resources from that agreed with the designer or any other resource area. It is often the case that many of the smaller financial or resource problems will be sorted out directly, by the designer within the design budget, or between the designer and the production associate. The production accountant will, in turn, keep the producer informed of the overall production costs.

Director
The designer works very closely with the director (who gives the production its creative urge, drive and identity) and will want to do everything possible to meet the director's requests. At the same time, it is the producer who has an overall budget for the production that covers all aspects of the creative process. This dual interest provides the designer with what is sometimes euphemistically called the creative tension that is set up between explosive and free-flowing creative demands on the one hand and the restrictions imposed by financial limits on the other.

Production accountant and production associate
The other members of the production team who work with the designer on budgetary matters are the production accountant and the production associate (on smaller programmes the production manager or even producer's assistant).

The production accountant generally works on location productions and is there to keep a tight grip on the cash flow and to provide a control centre in the middle of the unit. This control process will be concerned with timesheets, overtime, expenses and cash expenditure, as well as constant monitoring of budgets and the effecting of any necessary adjustments.

The production associate performs a similar but different task, and works very closely with the producer on financial and resources matters and is usually concerned with several productions simultaneously, as is the production accountant who is usually engaged specifically for one of the bigger productions. The production associate and the production accountant are both key points of contact for the designer during the realisation period, when adjustments may be necessary to the finances and resources of individual budgets.

Chapter 6

The Production Begins

The planning meeting

The director takes the opportunity at the planning meeting to explain to the assembled team what the intentions are for the camera rehearsal, recording or shoot, to discuss the problems which need to be resolved and to consult with those team members who may have an overlapping problem. In this way, the main problems encountered in the initial planning stages can be resolved at an early enough stage so that alterations can be easily incorporated. In turn these amendments can be included in the final studio or location plan, so that the agreed position reached at the planning meeting is recorded for every-one to see.

Briefing specialist contractors and suppliers with con-struction manager and production buyer

By this stage, the designer will have finalised the drawings and the projected costs and will be ready to concentrate on the final preparations involving the monitoring of progress of the many component parts of the programme design.

It is always a good idea to contact personally the various workshops, contractors and specialist suppliers in order to deliver a brief to supplement the final drawings. Much of the scenic requirement in television is of a repetitive nature, and can be safely conveyed through a drawing with notes and references provided, but also there is the need for items which are essential 'one-offs' and have to be made specially for the production — usually at a fraction of the cost it would have taken to develop and make an original object. In these cases there is bound to be much to discuss in order to achieve the best results. It is advisable to carry out these meetings together with the construction manager and/or the production buyer, so that they are party to the same conversations and will be in a better position to take a decision at some later stage if the designer is absent.

Finished plans of studio or location(s)

When the drawings have been finalised and sent to the con-tractors, a finished plan can be issued to the production team.

This may take the form of a studio plan (or plans depending on the complexity of the production), or a series of location plans showing the different settings and planned shots and what is being treated and what are the props planned for dressing. The word 'finished' plan is used deliberately, as there is likely to be a *final* plan at a later stage, following the technical run-through at the end of the rehearsal period when final adjustments to the setting and plans are made prior to the studio or shoot.

Another important reason for the issue of the finished plan is to provide the AFM with detailed information from which to mark out the sets on the rehearsal room floor. This makes clear what all the different elements are and usually involves the provision of a simple card model. There have been many classic mis-understandings in the past when, for example, half way through the rehearsal period it has been discovered that the archway through which an entrance was being made turns out to be a fireplace!

Read-through at rehearsal room
As soon as the rehearsal room is marked up, the read-through takes place. This involves the first full gathering of the cast, production team, writer and usually the costume and make-up designers as well as the production designer. The designer will have prepared finished models, sketches and plans so that, whether the production is recording in a studio or on location, the cast and production team can have the best possible idea of how the sets will look when the shoot takes place.

This first meeting with the full cast is always a fascinating experience for the designer. Faces and people become char-acters that so far have existed only on the page of the script and in the mind. Seeing the cast together in the same room for the first time can also be very revealing of the director's intentions on treatment and emphasis, and this in its turn can lead a designer into slightly different directions particularly in the area of prop selection and the opportunity of choosing items that reflect more closely the physical attributes of the character concerned. Similarly, the first time the script is heard is equally important; different emphases, inflections and interpretations can reveal other aspects of a character, as well as confirming those about which everyone agrees. For the designer, then, this experience at the read-through can provide a very fertile source of ideas concerned with the finer points of detail, dressing and interpretation.

Monitoring progess during preparation period

At this stage of the production, all work initiated by the designer (scenery, properties, specialist work, effects, CAD, etc) will be under way, and the continuing task is to monitor its progress while at the same time keeping abreast of any changes that might arise from the rehearsals.

It is essential to keep in close touch with the AFM whose job it is to note all the moves, actions, prop requirements, positions, and re-settings that are plotted during rehearsal. Inevitably the ideas developed originally by the designer and director as possible camera shots and movements do change as they are developed further by the actors. In order to obtain certain shots and positions, the size and shape of props, and occasionally even scenic items (doors swinging the other way or a hinged flat to swing), have to be changed to facilitate a camera move or a particularly critical shot. At this late stage it is important that information is conveyed from the AFM to the designer as quickly as possible as changes carried out before the build or acquisition has taken place can reduce extra costs by a significant amount.

Props are less of a problem in one sense, because they may at that stage not have been finally chosen and can be changed, but they can also present problems when requests emerge from the rehearsal for specific sized pieces of furniture. During outside rehearsal, the selected furniture is rarely available and consequently stand-in pieces have to be used. These substitutes often bear little relation to the props the designer has in mind for the studio. However, their size affects actors' moves which become built into the action. Problems then occur when the rehearsal prop turns out to be of a size that is not (or has never been) manufactured; this is particularly true of historical furniture styles in period plays, but also happens with modern furniture.

Contact with the production buyer is vital in order to relay these items of information and for the designer to be able to keep in touch with running prop costs. This is always a difficult area, and one which requires the closest contact between the designer, buyer, AFM and others involved.

Problems that could not be foreseen do occur and may call for radical changes of direction which sometimes require additional funds. If no alternative solution can be found and additional funds are not forthcoming, then the problem may only be solved by cutting back on existing requirements, which will mean involving the director and perhaps the producer.

The construction manager is another key figure in the final stages of preparation who will be checking to see that the work progresses according to plan and that all the component parts are co-ordinated towards completion at the correct moment. Depending upon the scale of the project, the designer will probably want to visit the contractor on a number of occasions during the building process. This will be for the initial briefing and to run-through the drawings, at the early stage of building, towards the end of the process as finishes are being applied, and then for final approval before the sets are cleared and transported to the studio or location. The problems that may occur are to do with matters of detail that have arisen during the actual building of the set; such points of detail need to be resolved by the designer who will have to choose the most appropriate alternative.

When shooting on location, the construction manager will be taken up with the preparation of a number of locations as dictated by the shooting schedule, so that once the shoot starts there are always a sufficient number of locations and sets ready to be shot when required. This could involve pre-fabricated workshop construction but quite possibly will mean only location craft work (involving carpenters, painters, plasterers and perhaps scenic artists) being carried out in the chosen locations. Again, the designer will need to keep in close touch with the progress of the work and be on hand to deal with any unforeseen difficulties that may arise.

Also, the main contractor or construction manager will be maintaining close contact with the specialist sub-contractors involved to ensure timed completion of their particular contributions. When specialist contractors are involved, time is often the most important element to be aware of when monitoring their progress as the problems they are solving are, by their nature, likely to be 'one-off' rather than part of an existing pattern. The designer will also have been maintaining appropriate contact with CAD and other specialist units like design effects or post-production preparation.

Attend the technical run
The technical run is a run-through of the production at the end of the rehearsal period, usually a day or so before the actual shoot or recording and is arranged for the specific purpose of covering the technical aspects of the production, so that lighting and sound, design, costume and make-up can make final assessments and adjustments before the shoot takes place. The actors usually present a walk-through and save their performances for the producer's run later in the day.

This provides the ideal opportunity for the team to make final notes and confer together before the shoot begins, in order to make the recording or filming run as smoothly as possible. A good example of this is the last-minute conference between the designer and AFM to ensure that all the changes that have occurred at the rehearsal are first of all known about and then provision made for them.

On film or location, there is the recce when the director and designer show the lighting camera operator the locations that are being prepared and the basic shots that are being proposed.

DESIGNER ISSUES FINAL STUDIO/LOCATION PLAN

fter the technical run, the designer can issue the final plan for studio or location. This is a vital piece of information for nearly everyone on the production team as it reflects the position reached at the end of the technical run and includes the results of the various consultations that have taken place. It is therefore the latest and most accurate information available, presented in plan form. In addition, some members of the team take the information and add their own items before passing it on to their respective support staff to be worked on.

Construction and setting crews

The plan provides accurate information with which to pre-set the scenery in the studio, often when the designer is occupied elsewhere. It positions precisely the sets and any major items of studio equipment that require accurate pre-setting while the studio or location is still relatively accessible and easy to work.

In a complicated set up, there may be scaffold rigs, steelwork or rostra as well as floors to be laid and painted. In this case there would be more than one plan used in order to separate out the different layers of information and the work processes involved. This is another situation where computer-aided design (CAD) can come into its own by easily producing several plans, each slightly different, showing layered information, all of which will speed up the pre-setting operation. Also there may be more than one plan needed if sets are to be re-built and props re-set to meet the requirements of continuity and discontinuous recording within the shooting schedule.

Properties

The position of furniture items and small prop dressings as well as drapes and soft furnishings, carpets and tapestries should be noted down, especially when the designer's presence cannot be guaranteed throughout the pre-setting period.

Cameras

In the case of a video studio shoot the production manager will add camera positions and cabling points to the final plan, which is usually then re-issued on a more limited distribution, so that the camera crew can use it when cabling up at the beginning of rehearsal.

Sound

Similarly, boom positions will be added by the production manager so that on arrival in the studio everyone knows where the technical equipment is to be placed initially and through the subsequent positions.

Visual effects and/or specialist contractors

When working with visual effects, specialist contractors, flying wire experts, etc, it is advisable for the designer to liaise with the specialist concerned to make sure that adequate provision has been made for facilities and studio space. Studio floor space needs to be allocated by the designer, as well as other facilities such as scenic hoists, beams, power and mechanical services.

Final visits to main contractor, sub-contractors and prop makers

Between the technical run and the pre-set operation, the designer will be making final visits to the main contractor or sub-contractors and prop-makers in order to accept their respective pieces of work before they are transported to the shoot. If the work is taking place *in situ* at the location, then the designer will finally approve at any convenient time before the shoot.

Studio or location pre-setting period

One of the main concerns for a designer during the final build-up prior to the shoot is to establish, together with the construction manager, the allocation and prioritising of work. There may have been changes made to the shooting schedule necessitated by problems emerging at the technical run, meaning that the order of setting needs changing to reflect the new recording schedule, especially in the case of rehearse-record, when it is essential to know which sets are required first. This same principle applies whether the production is being

design/construction/props shooting schedule

date	JANUARY		29TH	30TH	31ST	FEB 1ST	2ND	3RD
construction	set		FRONT DOOR		← GARAGE AND STABLES →			
	strike			FRONT DOOR TRAVEL				
props	dress		FRONT DOOR		TRAVEL BACK			
	strike			FRONT DOOR TRAVEL				
shoot			HALL & LANDING (STAGE)	TRAVEL	DAY OFF			CAM RECCE
scene no.			4	13				

construction location shooting schedule/budget

week ending	FEBRUARY 3RD	basic hours	overtime hours x 1.5	overtime hours x 2	total hours for week	cash figure
	SUPERVISOR	40	22½	—	62½	£
	CARPENTER	40	22½	—	62½	£
	STAGEHAND	40	22½	—	62½	£
	PAINTER (1)	40	22½	18	80½	£
	PAINTER (2)	40	22½	18	80½	£
	totals					£

week ending	FEBRUARY 10TH	basic hours	overtime hours x 1.5	overtime hours x 2	total hours for week	cash figure
	SUPERVISOR	40	24	—	64	
	CARPENTER	40	24	—	64	
	STAGEHAND	40	24	—	64	
	PAINTER (1)	40	24	—	64	
	PAINTER (2)	40	24	—	64	
	PAINTER (DAILY)	24	18	—	42	
	totals					£

made in a large electronic studio or is out on location with a number of different set-ups and sets being built or dressed.

The phasing and scheduling of the entire pre-set involves careful co-ordination between the construction manager and the scaffolders, steelworkers, craftsmen, electricians and props to ensure the most effective use of the time and space available. Gradually as the different parts of the jigsaw fall into place, the preparation (that is the building, painting, lighting, assembly and dressing with props of all the sets in the studio or on location) is completed and gradually they become ready for camera rehearsal.

Usually there is considerable patching up of scenery to be carried out by craftsmen when it has had to be transported from the originating workshop or contractor. The construction and floor painting activities are followed by the careful positioning of furniture, small props, drapes and soft goods into their designated positions.

STUDIO/SHOOTING DAY(S)
Having completed the pre-setting, construction and prop dressing in all its aspects, the next phase is the actual shooting or recording of the production. Whether or not the shoot takes place in an electronic studio, on video or on film at a location, there are certain basic activities and similarities in procedure that occur.

Blocking
The initial camera rehearsal period is taken up with blocking, where the actors' and camera moves are rehearsed individually before the complete sequence is run as a camera rehearsal. The moves of artists and cameras can be broken down and adjusted to suit the action, camera script, lighting, sound and design.

During blocking it is very important that the designer is watching carefully and is available next to camera or at the director's side, as planned shots can be easily lost or compromised simply by a camera happening to start off from a position that is different from the one the designer and director had in mind when originally planning. Equally, those key props, architectural features or lighting effects in a set that have been planned to be seen in a specific manner may need some attention and adjustment in order that the conditions are right to show them to the best effect.

Camera rehearsal

Immediately following the blocking procedure there will usually be a camera rehearsal, the purpose of which is to run the sequence or sections that have been blocked to see that they can be achieved satisfactorily up to speed, consecutively and without any further problems. Again, the designer needs to watch carefully to see whether or not further adjustment is required, particularly in the positioning of props, when the sequence is run up to speed and the framing of the picture is more difficult to achieve. This problem can sometimes be helped by the designer dressing a prop 'into the shot' rather than 'on to the set'.

Run-through

In a studio situation this means a rehearsal as near complete as possible of the whole show and with only the minimum of interruption. This obviously applies only in those situations where an entire show is being shot in one piece rather than in a series of one-off shots or of short, rehearse-record sequences.

Again, it is important for the designer to be aware of how the pictures work when the show is being run through as a complete entity, as there can be a significant difference between the framing of shots lined up in rehearsal and those which come up in the middle of a long sequence.

Pre-recordings

It might reasonably be assumed from the above that there is a sequential order of recording, but of course there are many times when this is not the case. The first of these is known as pre-recording, when certain sections of a production may be recorded at the beginning of the day rather than in its natural position in the script. This can occur for a variety of reasons, ranging from major costume and make-up changes (for instance to convey ageing and passage of time), to major set changes and re-dressings or for the recording of effects sequences. In all these examples the basis of the decision is that too much time would be taken by attempting the changes within the context of the real time running order, so these items are isolated and may be taken at the beginning or (contrary to the title) at the end of the period. This would then be referred to as rehearse-record or discontinuous recording.

Rehearse-record

Today, most shooting in drama is carried out on a rehearse-record basis, that is to say having the set (and all other aspects of the realisation team's work) completely prepared and ready so that immediately after the blocking and camera rehearsal that particular scene or section is recorded immediately.

As long as the necessary preparation by the realisation team can be completed in time before the blocking and camera rehearsal, then the system works well. If, however, the preparation is not fully complete, then it may mean that an unfinished or compromised picture is recorded early in the schedule which then cannot be corrected without creating further problems of discontinuity. Rehearse-record also limits the opportunity for any more than minor adjustments to setting and dressing, costume and make-up, lighting and sound. However, the trend is now clearly established to shoot in this fashion and with it goes an acceptance that if such adjustments are necessary then the necessary preparation or alteration will have to take place within the actual shooting time.

Watching pictures

Throughout the studio or shooting day, the designer's main task could be said to be watching the pictures and images emerging from the blocking and camera rehearsals, and then making the necessary adjustments to set and prop dressings, while nego-tiating with lighting, sound, cameras, costume and make-up to try to solve problems that may have occurred and which are preventing the realisation of planned shots.

This may sound a relatively simple task and indeed a pleasant one, being the culmination and final monitoring of all the pre-planning and preparation that has been taking place for so long. However, the reality invariably turns out to be something different and the majority of designers would probably say that in practice they manage to get very little 'picture watching' done.

The reasons for this are many. So often, because of the transient nature of television and film and the speed with which so much of the work has to be carried out, there is bound to be human error which, in turn, leads to problems occurring that could not have not been anticipated or planned for. This is particularly so in the design area where there are almost endless possibilities always available, the final choice being dependent upon the director's and designer's wishes but, in the end, a purely pragmatic acceptance that time is about to run out and a decision *has* to be made.

In a studio recording the designer perhaps has a better chance to watch pictures, although this depends on the size of produc-tion and the extent of the assistance available. For while monitoring is taking place it means that other activities are severely restricted. If a designer works on a smaller production with no other assistance available, then it may be necessary to forego the pleasure of watching the pictures.

LOCATION SHOOTING
On location, the production designer will invariably have assist-ance available in one form or another (art director or design assistant, construction manager and team, production buyer and prop crew), but the basic decision to be made together with the director is whether the production designer stays next to

camera during the shoot, or whether it is the art director or assistant who carries out this task. This depends very much on the individuals concerned and arguments can be put forward for both arrangements.

Working ahead of the camera
Depending upon the complexity of the preparation work taking place in locations ahead of the current shoot, the production designer may feel it is unnecessary to be there, particularly if the shoot is relatively simple and there is not a large amount of design involvement. In this case the art director or assistant will easily be able to deal with any problems that might arise in terms of dressing and picture composition by keeping in close touch with the lighting camera operator, and often by arranging to have a video link run off the camera to make monitoring much easier than having to look through the viewfinder each time.

Working with the camera
If a shot is complicated enough to need some adjustments to ensure that it works satisfactorily, then the arrangement may well be reversed. Some directors much prefer to see the designer at their side during the shoot as an immediate reference point to the plans they made together in the early stages of the production. Others prefer that the designer is working ahead to guarantee that everything is well prepared before the camera arrives and decisions have to be made.

Self-sufficiency
Once a unit leaves base for a location shoot it is basically 'on its own', and compared with a studio production the success or failure of the enterprise rests squarely on the shoulders of the production and realisation teams. They are not supported by the back-up systems available to a studio-based production when it is usually possible (admittedly at a cost) to switch resources and re-allocate effort to deal with emergency problems. Consequently, the team on location has to rely on its own resources and initiative. The composition of teams is very important so that people with the best attitudes and personalities are chosen. For the production designer this consists of

an art director or design assistant, construction manager and team, production buyer and the prop crew, all of whom need to have the same approach and be ready to work closely together under pressure.

Re-scheduling requirements

On location the production designer has to meet two main requirements — firstly to be well planned, imaginative and intuitive and, secondly, to be ready and able to change plans quickly while at the same time somehow retaining the feel of the original planned creative style and approach. Severe weather conditions or the sudden indisposition of an actor or some other similar problem can easily cause the shooting schedule to be re-examined urgently. This can be a complicated operation for the designer and support team. For unless the unit can carry around with it all the sets and props that are still to be shot there is always bound to be a complex problem of logistics to solve when planning a re-shoot or re-schedule. Usually, there will be some form of base established while away on location — even if it is of the moving variety in the back of an articulated lorry, but it can often be one of the main locations which will provide storage facilities and enable the unit to shoot in smaller locations or individual sets.

Continuity

Once a schedule has to be re-organised at short notice, it is easy to overlook the element of continuity required for props and scenery. Also, it may be difficult to remember the details of a set that has been shot and apparently finished with, only to find later that it has to be reinstated. So continuity notes are crucially important for the designer at each stage of the shoot, and instant cameras provide excellent information that go a long way to covering this eventuality and can save valuable time in spooling through tape to grab a frame.

POST PRODUCTION

After the shoot or studio recording has been completed, the next phase is post production when final editing takes place.

Often this will not involve the designer at all, except in those cases where planned design effects have been involved. When this happens the designer's presence is necessary in the final stages in order to explain the original intention of the effect, plus any problems that may have occurred along the way and which require some attention or adjustment in the final edit. There may well be the need to add further touches with a digital paint system to give a desired effect, especially when assembling multi-image composite pictures. Deciding finally how to treat matte lines and joins in order either to hide them or to emphasise them to heighten the required effect may be a priority. Even with a relatively simple matte shot or inlay, the designer needs to be able to assess the picture as a whole, particularly in relation to tonal values which can so easily become distorted in digital manipulation and which require further adjustment. Without this intervention, some of the electronic effects can easily become too conspicuous rather than unobtrusive.

Chapter 7

New Technologies in Production Design

At the present time, there are many developments taking place in the technical areas surrounding production design that call for a different design approach and a greater awareness of new possibilities. The whole area of image creation and picture manipulation is one that the designer should be very much aware of as part of the overall artistic palette available to the production. These new technologies are constantly being produced.

This is a new phenomenon and calls for a different approach. For many years designers have been spending the majority of their efforts in the realisation of scenic effects, sets and properties, whereas now it is possible to manipulate images electronically using digital effects rather than timber, paint and props. Suddenly the whole world of visual relationships has been opened up in a more direct manner than was ever possible before. Designers can use their visual training to best effect by having available direct control over the picture they are instrumental in creating.

CAD
A brief reference to computers, digital video effects and computer graphics has already been made in this book, and here it is intended to look in more detail at CAD (computer aided design). This is the system that is most closely linked with the production designer, who is concerned with 2-D and 3-D images, with the draughting of plans and elevations and the production of perspective camera views. More important are the fast developing possibilities and links between CAD, video and graphic images that are emerging at the present time.

Early experience
When the BBC acquired an experimental CAD system for television designers back in 1984, it was extremely difficult for computer systems (other than the most complex and expensive ones) to begin to meet the needs of the television designers. Much development work was needed in order to achieve the simple objectives of a moveable camera viewpoint that would produce perspective views of the camera shot to given lens

specifications and aspect ratios. The production of drawings and plans were well advanced at that time, but links between them and the camera views were not at all easy if indeed they were possible at all

Recent development

Between these early days and the present time an enormous amount of further development has taken place. More recently there has been a fundamental change in direction in the whole computer world brought about by the change from larger, more complex computers to smaller personal computers which nowadays can frequently carry out more tasks and with far more accessible operating systems.

Now it is possible for non-computer experts to be able to acquire a personal computer system which allows them to achieve these basic objectives and far more besides. And there are still more developments both to the hardware and the software programmes taking place all the time.

Some basic principles (and misconceptions)

It is frequently argued that computers will save time on, say, draughting, and therefore jobs and money. Often staff reductions are argued on that basis. Either way there is a danger of misunderstanding what it is that computers can and will do best in given circumstances — especially in design.

Although computers can carry out many tasks far quicker than most people can produce by hand, there are still certain aspects of work that are better carried out manually because of operational demands. In production design a computer might be at its most effective when making changes to existing information, for example, studio plans (which of course have been entered into the computer's memory in the first place), that are required to be issued regularly and with amended information each time. On the other hand a single, once-only, original drawing of whatever level of complexity that is required in a very short time may not warrant the time necessary to create it in the computer in the first place.

A fully trained designer can, in given circumstances produce drawings and plans much faster than conventional methods. These given circumstances include access to a library of stock items (that will be used and re-used in the future) so that no item needs to be drawn twice, which means that the computer's re-assembly of sets built from stock items can be cut down by a large percentage. The storage of files on disk and instant access to them saves on time and space over conventional methods. Also, automatic dimensioning and pre-written notes add to the potential time saving, as does the increased clarity of the finished drawing, which is of particular benefit to the construction and setting crews.

So, *owning a computer does not automatically mean that it always provides the quickest way to do everything*, and the designer must decide whether or not to use it based on the merits of each situation.

Most computer consultants would agree that if there is one recurring problem that is common to nearly all prospective computer set-ups it is that once the computer system has been decided upon, *insufficient time is normally allowed for training*. This can prove to be the same false economy whether it concerns an individual designer or a whole section or department. For some reason the conviction behind acquiring the computer system in the first place does not extend far enough to include sufficient training and familiarisation, despite the fact that this could, and often does, jeopardise the whole enterprise. Once properly trained, however, the greater proficiency of the users invariably leads to a greater awareness of the further potential of the system and the realisation of additional benefits.

Another example of time saving by the computer is of a collective nature. When for instance, a complicated and large-scale project is being prepared, a computer presentation (plans, perspectives, rendered and lit camera viewpoints, composite images or frames grabbed from video and treated with a paint system) — despite the time taken to prepare it — can still produce a large saving of time by demonstrating and explaining the project simply and quickly in a manner that is not open to debate, as is the case with freehand sketches. In this way the production as a whole benefits from CAD and not simply the designer.

Design effects

Design effects have been used and developed in television over the years. At first theatrical techniques of gauze painting were used, then foreground model shots or glass shots to extend the scale of the scenic elements in the studio or on location, followed by the advent of inlay and overlay which allowed more sophisticated blending of images and effects. Digital paint systems now allow the production designer to work on complex individual shots before or after the main shoot or recording with the intention of incorporating them during the final edit. Also, portable video cameras allow designers to carry out recces for design effects shots, so that they can work on the still frames with a digital paint system and present the director with a very good idea of how the design effect will look.

Links with computer graphics systems

In Japan, the NHK CAD system is already linked with a computer graphics software package, so that the two can be used together, yet still carry out their respective tasks separately. The architectural draughting capability for plans and elevations and the particular modelling capabilities of the CAD system — providing basic information concerning dimensions, volume, weight, etc, of the item concerned — can be linked to the surface modelling and highly sophisticated rendering and animation capabilities of the graphic system. The links between the graphic images in a title sequence and the scenic elements that need to be visually related and described accurately in order to be physically built, are of special value to a designer who may be responsible for the complete design of a programme, including graphics and the set.

Links with production computers

If the designer is using a CAD system which is compatible with the production associate/manager/accountant's computer, then it is possible to aspire to computer aided production as well as computer aided design. Design information and production information that require the same source, e.g. up-to-date shooting schedule, can be constantly up-dated by networking the different computer terminals or workstations, so that the designer or production team can always see the latest schedule and its implications for the realisation team. Similarly, cost monitoring (e.g. of the design and construction budget) can easily take place, and (in a larger organisation particularly) this flow of information can be very important in monitoring and controlling costs over a wide range of productions. Both production offices and designers can also make use of word processing, database, spreadsheets and project planning programmes for quicker and easier communication.

Possibilities and future trends

Future possibilities for the use of computers by production designers in television is limited only by the nature of the projects being designed and the money that they or their organisations can justify spending. In terms of future possibilities and trends, the scope is enormous; the converging interests of the broadcasting, telecommunications and computing industries mean that computer graphics will continue to develop, driven by the demand and interests of three different areas of industry.

Within television, it is the links between the different computer systems, that will provide the interesting developments; for example, CAD 3D data linked to 3D real time computer graphics for virtual reality images; synthetic or 'electric' sets into which presenters or real time computer animation characters can be integrated. Also it is possible to connect 3D CAD data to other engineering systems such as lighting, in order to develop simulation systems so that lighting levels and settings can largely be determined in advance. These links once set up can obviously work two ways and the whole idea of networking between the various members of a production team is likely to become commonplace quite soon, bringing with it limitless possibilities.

High definition and wide screen television
The likely financial investment in television equipment and the changes in technique required by the introduction of high definition television are so great that it is inevitable that progress is slow. However, despite existing differences of standards and equipment around the world, there is a distinct feeling that HDTV is here to stay, although it is difficult to predict how quickly the system will spread.

The arrival of HD and wide screen television with a different aspect ratio and much sharper definition than current television systems may be viewed by designers as a mixed blessing rather an unquestionable benefit. They will need to provide a higher standard and quality of finish to withstand the scrutiny of the HDTV camera with its larger and sharper picture and they will need to pay exceptional attention to both sets and props, which will be seen for the first time on television in their actual state of finish and repair. Smudges, scratches, bad joins, creased fabrics, make-up joins, damaged props and wilting greenery will suddenly be exposed in their full glory (or horror), whereas in the past the television camera and the quality of picture it produces, has effectively disguised these blemishes and thus avoided the problem. This attention to detail and better finishes will inevitably attract additional costs — much more akin to those demanded when building sets to be shot on 35mm film and shown on a large screen; there may also be additional time taken in preparing or altering such finishes during the shoot. Already HDTV is being used in some circumstances as a more cost effective means of producing visual effects by transferring from 35mm film to tape, digitally processing the images and then returning them to 35mm film. This can prove to be cheaper than the cost of producing optical effects on film.

Paradoxically, the high definition picture may well mean the viewer being able to see in greater detail those things that perhaps might better not be seen at all! HDTV invites viewers to look at things literally through new eyes and presents them with a mass of information about which they had previously been unaware and unconcerned. While the larger, sharper image will be a marvellous improvement if the subject matter is, for example, a sporting event, a drama director needing mood lighting and atmosphere could be forgiven for preferring to use film with its different quality of softness and light.

However, these reservations are very reminiscent of the arguments put forward when television changed from 405 to 625 lines in the '60s and given time the industry will surely develop the necessary techniques and provide the resources to service the new picture when it is needed. Also, directors, designers and viewers will quickly adapt to the new facility once productions become available in sufficient quantity.

Designers, therefore, can look forward to the development from a slightly detached viewpoint and simply wait for the opportunity to be asked to work in the new style afforded by the different picture ratio. Their existing production experience and skills will still be relevant, but the enlarged and wider picture will allow new and exciting possibilities when composing pictures, both single camera and composite images. Once established as a regular part of the television scene, HDTV will offer new challenges and visual possibilities for directors and designers alike.

EVALUATING THE DESIGN CONTRIBUTION

If their work is to develop in a significant and genuine progression, then it is essential for designers to be true to themselves and to take on the responsibility of evaluating their own work. This is not an easy task, but one which is crucial to the continuing development of the creative and artistic mind. In a purely commercial sense, the designer's employer or patron — often the producer or director — may well be satisfied with the design as carried out and for the given price. But instinctively the designer will want to evaluate the work not simply from a financial aspect but from a purely design perspective, to ask whether certain elements could have been carried out better, differently perhaps, but still within the given financial and other parameters. The truly committed designer will always rely on self-criticism, self-analysis, continuing self-education and consequently self-belief for future work. It is important to know what went right and what went wrong, why and how to improve or avoid such elements in projects for the future. The process of continuing self-education does not, of course, exclude listening to the comments of others, but detailed analysis of what is a continuous process of design and realisation, arrived at by a series of qualitative decisions, poses a series of inter-related questions that committed designers will want to examine themselves.

How did the designer's contribution work for the production?

In developing a design brief?

- Did the design style serve the production well?
- Were the overall conceptual requirements identified?
- Did the design help the actors/artists in interpreting the script/score?
- Did the design offer an appropriate visual metaphor?
- Was the approach consistent throughout?

In the origination of design ideas?

- How well were design options explored?
- Was the widest range of options new and old, as well as specialist expertise, explored?

In translating these ideas into practical proposals ?

- Were the proposals fully and clearly presented?
- Were the proposals readily understood and agreed by the director and team?
- In producing specifications and drawings?
- Were the specifications clear, comprehensive and on time?

In establishing the necessary budget and resource?

- Was the design budget comprehensive in its coverage?
- Were any items overlooked?

In monitoring and controlling the budget and resources?

- Was the design team properly briefed to schedule and monitor the cash and resources?
- Did the production come in on budget? If not, what lessons are to be learned?

In commissioning the necessary contractors suppliers and specialists?

- Did all the contributors have adequate briefings and specifications?
- Did they have sufficient time to carry out the work?
- Were the best people chosen to do the job?

In realising and achieving the design?

- Could the scenery and props have been better made?
- Were all the key shots and sequences achieved? If not, why not?
- Did the design team allocate and prioritise work effectively?
- Was the design concept realised to the designer's satisfaction?

These questions are intended to be no more than a skeleton of the de-briefing that ideally should take place within the design team, and sometimes with the director and producer, at the end of a production. The intention is to review the effectiveness of decisions taken at various stages through the realisation process, so that better decisions may be made next time. Self-questioning and evaluation should produce a process of self-education and a learning opportunity that continues through the designer's career and if pursued with commitment and energy will surely lead to better designs and productions.

Chapter 8

Learning about
Television Design

EXPANDING HORIZONS

It has to be said that the choice and availability of training for today's aspiring television designers is limited and its provision is unlikely to alter very much in the short term. There are perhaps three or four full-time courses at degree or comparable level in colleges, schools or universities around the country, which provide the possibility of carrying out a television design project as part of an associated course in subjects such as interior or exhibition design. Also, there are some evening classes, usually run by practising television designers, that provide limited familiarisation training for those who already may be design or art graduates in another discipline, but who are hoping to enter television.

The providers of training in the past, the BBC and ITV companies, carried out this task mainly by 'on-the-job' training, in-house courses and external specialist training days. Today they are all gradually withdrawing from this field because of lack of funds and a shortage of people to carry out the training as staff numbers are cut back to minimal levels. It is extremely unlikely that design departments nowdays will be able any longer to underwrite the costs, resources and time required for in-house design training.

How will design training differ from previous generations?
It can be argued that in future the nature of training for television design will hardly change at all. The reason for saying this is that the academic and other training establishments that existed before this new situation still operate, although they often come under threat of one sort or another. Also, if one is frank, it has to be admitted that in the past the amount of design training provided by the television companies was not enormous. The real basis of training would have been obtained already through a degree course in any one of many different design or art disciplines, or sometimes a BTech qualification, which led to selected graduates having a demonstrable awareness and aptitude for working in television. This acquisition of art or design skills would be followed up by 'on-the-job' training, or just occasionally a special training scheme. For example when BBC2 opened in 1964 the BBC had suddenly to field

twenty-four new designers and so a crash training scheme was essential.

In this sense it can be said that little has changed and little is likely to change. The majority of designers will still train in the subject of their choice and usually to degree level and will at some stage discover, if they have not done so already, the inclination to work in television. A minority will find their way into the small number of full time courses and avail themselves of specialist and usually (but not always) post graduate training.

However they may be trained, the key attributes in a television designer can be said to be:

- A lively visual imagination
- The ability to express this in various media — from drawing to video
- A commitment to television design
- A wide interest in people and the arts throughout history
- The necessary interpersonal skills and ability to deal with all the people involved in the television making process.

It is obviously possible to acquire these attributes and skills and experience both inside and outside the existing further education framework and without necessarily having attended one of the few specialist courses for television design.

THE PLACE OF S/NVQs IN TRAINING FOR TELEVISION DESIGNERS

Although the picture painted of future training for television designers is not very optimistic, there is a new and important series of developments taking place which undoubtedly will have an effect on it. The recently instituted National and Scottish Vocational Qualifications set up by the Government with the support of the three main political parties, the Confederation of British Industry and the Trades Union Congress, already has the support and participation of one-hundred-and-sixty industries, and is intended to raise the standards of competence by training more people to a higher level. The S/NVQs are based on standards developed by industry and are designed to give people better access to opportunities offered by training and qualifications.

S/NVQs in the television industry
Within the film, broadcast and video industry, the Skillset project was established following the Skill Search Report two years previously which recommended the development of common standards of competence. This process took place during 1991 and 1992 and involved some two-hundred professionals from all sectors of film and broadcasting who agreed to pool their wide experience of the industry to define the performance needs of the industry as a whole by identifying the levels of competence required. The working groups were asked to put job titles and descriptions to the back of their minds and concentrate instead on the results they expected to see achieved.

After the setting of standards, the natural progression will be the awarding of qualifications that enable individuals to prove — and potential employers to recognise — that a certain level of competence has been achieved. Skillset's standards have been formulated in such a way that they fit in with the National Vocational Qualifications System, which leads to the award of NVQs (National Vocational Qualifications) or SVQs (Scottish Vocational Qualifications).

These qualifications will go very much in hand with the notion of designers and artists working in television, but without necessarily having had training that is specific to television design. This situation is nothing new and has been occurring for the past twenty-five years at least. During this time, many people were working in television design (and of course other disciplines) gaining experience for which there was no formal recognition. This anomaly can be remedied by way of NVQs and SNVQs providing a way of verifying individuals' competence, so that it is no longer a case of who they know but of what they can do.

An extension of Skillset's remit has been its development into the Industry Training Organisation for Film, Broadcast and Video, which has three main aims:

- The provision of regularly up-dated information on employment and training within the industry
- The provision of increased training for the freelance and independent sectors
- The development of common standards of competence.

In future, therefore, the training of individual designers will probably take place much as it did in the past, but with the important distinction of the presence of these new qualifications as a means of recognising existing skills acquired already within the industry, and without necessarily having to embark on further training. In addition, and especially where further training may be necessary, there will be the added assistance of the Industry Training Organisation.

It will be seen that the design process and main stages of designing written about in the earlier part of this book has been described in a narrative sense, in order to provide a feeling of what it is like to design for television and to emphasise the important points to remember within that process. The Design Working Group of Skillset, on the other hand, has not been concerned as much with the question of how to do the job, as with a functional analysis of the design process, using the N/SVQ system of :

Units
A level of competence to be reached by an individual; this can be accredited separately and will form part of a qualification. So far, Skillset has identified over three-hundred units of competence.

Elements of competence
Units break down into elements which again define a duty or function which a person working in a given occupational area should be able to undertake satisfactorily.

Performance criteria
Statements against which a judgement can be made.

Range statements
The description of a range of activities, situations or contexts in which competence should be judged. This can include methods and equipment used as well as the type of production and whether it takes place in the studio or on location.

In this way, it is possible for the assessment and recognition of standards to be incorporated into the S/NVQ system. S/NVQs will mean that from an employer's point of view it will be easier to check that applicants have the competence needed and that it is independently verified. From the point of view of the training providers it will mean that the modular build-up of the qualifications together with the performance standards lend themselves to very precise targeting of training objectives.

From the individual's point of view it will be possible to gain nationally recognised qualifications, making it easier to move between industry sectors and even from one industry to another — if that individual happens to be a designer, then the wheel might just have turned full circle and the question will be posed once again "Where's the designer?"

FURTHER READING AND VIEWING

Production design in television depends very much on the designer having a thorough awareness of the work of the other members of the realisation team. When writing this book I have had in mind the books and videos already published by BBC Television Training. They make essential reading and provide the ideal accompaniments to this book on TV design; I have grouped them under the following broad headings:

BOOKS	VIDEOS
Studio Work	
Stand By Studio!	Television
Directing Situation Comedy	Script to Screen
Camera Mountings	Camera Mountings
TheTV Graphics Handbook	Graphic Design
	Graphics: A Guide to the Equipment
Wallchart: In the Studio	
Wallchart: Run to Record	
Location Work	
Shooting on Location	Single Camera Shooting
	The Basics
	An Ambitious Sequence
After Tea We'll do the Fight	Filming Action
	The Language of Film
	Part 1 Lenses & Light
	Part 2 The Soundtrack
	Part 3 Actors and the Camera
Wallchart: Out on Location	
Drama	
Making a Drama of It	
Special Effects	
Does the horse explode?	Vanity Fair: The Battlefield
	Electronic Effects
Music and Sound Effects	Music & Sound Effects for Television
News	
News! News!	The Making of the Six

BOOKS	**VIDEOS**
Documentaries	
From Script to Screen	The Structure of Documentaries
Outside Broadcasts	
A Right Royal Do	
Editing	
Editing Film and Videotape	Creative Editing
Narration and Editing	Television Narration & Editing
	The Language of Film
	Part 4 Post Production
Continuity	
Continuity Notes	Continuity & the Single Camera
	1. An Introduction
	2. Tricks of the Trade

Research
The Television Researcher's Guide
Teletalk: a Dictionary of Broadcasting Terms

Production Assistance
The Production Assistant's Survival Guide

Television Production
Television Training: Approaches to Production and Direction

Technical
High Definition Television for the Programme Maker

NB Please note that the above books are available to all members of the public. However, for copyright reasons the videos may only be purchased by training establishments.